THE RENEGADE REVOLUTIONARIES

Harold E. Bronson

New Star Books

ISBN 0-919888-53-4 (paper)
& 0-919888-54-2 (cloth)

New Star Books
2504 York Avenue
Vancouver 9, B.C.

Contents

Preface

Readers will not expect a complete study of the Fourth International in a volume of this size. Those who wish to pursue the subject further will find some guidance in the references provided.

The main purpose of this book is to examine the circumstances and ideological tendencies which explain the role of Trotskyism in the growing confrontation between imperialist countries and those still suffering from colonialism and neo-colonialism.

Why was the Fourth International the only major world organization to oppose the signing of the draft agreement for a Vietnamese ceasefire, which eventually resulted in the withdrawal of U.S. military forces?

Why did the Fourth seem to be demanding direct Chinese intervention in that war?

In future military confrontations of that kind, can we expect similar agitation from the Trotskyites and from the much larger New Left and neo-Trotskyite groups?

What political and economic consequences can we anticipate in view of the regular Trotskyite practice of working within social-democratic parties and trying to influence their approach to imperialism?

What common ground is there to support such liaisons?

In general, what is the Fourth International trying to do, and for whose benefit?

For this book I have selected and ex-

amined those parts of early and recent Trotskyite history which help to explain such questions. From that perspective, persistent patterns of thought and conduct emerge, from which we can readily assess Trotskyism's character and consequences.

Those patterns appear in the policies of an endless panorama of organizations. Some of these deny any allegiance to Trotskyism, as in the case of the "Independent Socialists" who became visible across Canada in 1975 as a regrouping of some "Waffle" elements. Identification of Trotskyism's basic characteristics should be useful in making appraisals of such organizations as they develop.

Source material for such a topic usually tends to be strongly biased. But it is generally safe to conclude that there will be a hard core of truth in the criticisms conceded by admirers, and in the merits admitted by opponents. Furthermore, criticisms of Trotsky by a contemporary like Lenin, whom the Fourth International claims as a supporter, should be regarded as having a relatively high degree of credibility. Accordingly, I have concentrated mainly on these more reliable sources.

I am grateful to those who provided constructive comments during the development of the manuscript.

HAROLD E. BRONSON

Saskatoon, Canada,
December, 1975.

Chapter I

WHY TROTSKYISM NEEDS ATTENTION

SUMMARY

The ideological conflict which developed between Trotsky and Lenin, and continued between Trotsky and Stalin, has survived those individuals. It has persisted because the struggles on which it was based have persisted - and intensified.

A new height in these contradictions was reached late in 1972 as world demand arose for the United States to sign the draft agreement ending its military presence in Viet Nam. World attention was then drawn to the fact that the only international ally of the U.S.-Saigon axis in its reluctance to sign was the Fourth International,[1] i.e. world Trotskyism.

Thus another twentieth century generation was made aware of the need to examine the background and connections of the Fourth International. The "New Left", many of whom have vigorously denied any fondness for Trotskyism, began to find that a good deal of common ground existed.

It also appears that the New Left and other neo-Trotskyite groups have much in common with the Soviet "revision" of Marxism-Leninism. Soviet revisionism, which began with Khrushchov, emerged like Trotskyism with attacks on Stalin. Other important similarities include the common rejection of national self-reliance, either before or after the attainment of socialist state power.

The most consistent opposition to Trotskyism, neo-Trotskyism and revisionism has come from the organizations which have successfully applied Mao Tse-tung's development of Marxism-Leninism. The accumulation of revolutionary theory by Marx, Lenin and Mao Tse-tung (MLM theory) has provided the basis for seizure and maintenance of state power in China,North Korea, Albania, Cambodia and Viet Nam. MLM principles also seem to prevail in Cuba, although the Soviet economic grip prevents open acknowledgement of that influence.

All of these governments have defined Trotskyism as an enemy. The reasons: 1) it has led people away from effective anti-imperialist activity; 2) it has led others into active sabotage of the liberation movements; and 3) it has created distrust of revolutionary processes among many who otherwise might have been supporters.

The Fourth International, which was established by Trotsky after he was banished from the Soviet Union, has moved in where-ever its radical rhetoric can win approval. For example,it found some acceptance within the "Waffle" wing of the Canadian New Democratic Party (NDP).

Actually, a neo-Trotskyite "New Left" faction eventually came to control a major fragment of the disintegrating Waffle. The faction's appeal was based on the individualism and dramatic appeals of imported

U.S. radicalism.

This neo-Trotskyite presence influenced the Waffle away from its original emphasis on national independence as the first essential step toward socialism. The neo-Trotskyites hampered the independence struggle by opposing specific anti-imperialist programs.

1) They opposed the struggle to free Canadian labour from AFL-CIO control.

2) They opposed the struggle to reduce U.S. influence in Canadian education.

3) They tried to distract the attention of farmers and consumers from the domination of Canadian agribusiness by U.S. cartels.

4) They sought to direct the people's wrath toward Canadian reactionaries and Canadian "imperialists".

Where superpower imperialism could not be ignored, the neo-Trotskyites persistently pointed to the "multi-national corporations" as the villains. They carefully avoided reference to the much more pertinent fact that in 1973, 10 of the largest 12 "multi-national" corporations were controlled in the U.S. None was Canadian. (See below, Chapter 5.)

Trotskyism has always refused to concentrate on the main oppressive force. Thus it has tended to encourage the dispersal of anti-imperialist ranks into many simultaneous battles against all enemies, large and small. Obviously the main enemy* must

---

*Liberation forces generally regard U.S.

approve of such a dispersal.

Trotsky pursued the same objective in Lenin's time.But the anti-imperialist forces now have an advantage in that they can evaluate Trotskyism on its record. Thus they can avoid a repetition of earlier setbacks attributable to its influence.

MAIN TEXT

The Bolshevik Revolution in Russia brought to world attention the name Leon Trotsky (a pseudonym for Lev Davidovich Bronstein). In Russia, as we shall see, he represented a class and an ideology which still affect twentieth century political economy.

The study of Trotsky's personal life therefore becomes important because he has been made a symbol by those who seek to promote his ideas and methods. The ideas and activities associated with Trotsky become particularly significant when major confrontations occur between the perpetrators and the victims of economic exploitation and military aggression.

TROTSKYISM OPPOSES THE VIET NAM CEASEFIRE

An important indication of the Fourth International's role in such confronta-

---

imperialism as the main enemy. Those who are more directly threatened by the new Soviet "social-imperialism" may be obliged to place the U.S.S.R. in that category.

tions appeared during the 1972-73 cease-fire negotiations between the Vietnamese liberation forces and the U.S.- Saigon axis. For several weeks before ordering the December bombing of North Viet Nam, President Nixon had refused to authorize signing the draft agreement.

Protests against that delay came from all the main areas of world opinion, with one exception. As Carl Davidson observed in the *Guardian* (New York):

> ...Nixon had one additional ally to set against this dramatic example of the international united front against U.S. imperialism - almost the entire Trotskyist movement. The Trotskyists too, were opposed to demanding that Nixon sign the treaty, urged that the agreement be scrapped, and claimed that it would violate the "right of self-determination of South Vietnam." They organized opposition to the demand within the U.S. anti-war movement, carried article after article in their press indicating that the treaty was a "sellout" and a "betrayal" of Vietnam's national rights and threatened to organize separate protests if the demand was made the principal slogan of the planned mass mobilizations....

Davidson went on to conclude that this showed again the Trotskyite characteristic of appearing "left" only in form, while remaining "thoroughly rightist in actuality."[2]

That assessment was supported by arguments put forward in the official Trotskyite press. Discussing the ceasefire proceedings in Viet Nam, the organ of the Trotskyite Socialist Workers' Party (SWP) in the United States opposed the treaty with the demand: "U.S. get out of all Southeast Asia immediately! No conditions!" And further:

> Moscow and Peking have been entertaining Nixon and making deals with him to strangle the Vietnamese revolution..They refused to provide the Vietnamese with the most modern fighter planes and anti-aircraft weapons needed for the defense against U.S. bombing attacks.[3]

That criticism was applicable to the U.S.S.R. but not to China. The U.S.S.R. had refused to give Viet Nam the latest fighters and missiles. But the Chinese had repeatedly emphasized their willingness to supply anything they had available, if requested. The Trotskyites could hardly have been unaware of the fact that China was not producing the most advanced fighters and anti-aircraft weapons.

What the Trotskyites were actually demanding of China was armed invasion of Indo-China. Quoting from SWP sources in the U.S., Carl Davidson concluded that they wanted a repetition of Chinese action in North Korea when MacArthur's army threatened the Chinese border. The Trotskyite definition of "adequate" aid from China, said Davidson, "boils down to China's giving the People's Liberation Army their marching orders."[4]

It will be observed as we examine the record more thoroughly that this support for uninvited army intervention by stronger powers is characteristic of Trotskyism, despite its calls for "national self-determination."

Exercising self-determination of a most effective kind, the Vietnamese did not call for the Chinese army. Their own military and political offensives forced the U.S. into negotiations which, far from being a sellout, proved to be a qualitative leap forward toward Vietnamese unity and independence.

The resistance to further U.S. intervention created by these combined offensives was enough,both in the U.S. and elsewhere, to ensure that President Ford could not renew that intervention. Thus conditions had been developed, by April,1975, for the total liberation of Viet Nam and Cambodia.

These events did not lead MLM theorists to assume that the U.S. had abandoned its goal of hegemony in South-East Asia and the rest of the Third World. But they did lead to the assurance that Vietnamese liberation strategy had scored a major success with the ceasefire agreements and the consequent withdrawal of U.S. forces.

That withdrawal, together with the denial of funds by Congress for further bombing of Cambodia and the general resistance to a renewal of American intervention in Viet Nam all showed the effectiveness of the military and political strategies of the Indo-Chinese patriots. So the Trotskyites were "wrong" in their campaign against the ceasefire agreement.

That is, they were wrong from the viewpoint of the Indo-Chinese people. They were right, however, from the perspective of those elements in U.S. society who want to maintain a military presence in those countries. The importance of this distinction will become more apparent as we examine the record of the Fourth International and the role which it continues to play in world affairs.

THE FOURTH'S ALL-OR-NOTHING DEMANDS DISCOURAGE AND DISCREDIT THE LEFT

The controversy over the cease-fire treaty showed up another typical feature of the Fourth International. That was the "all-or-nothing" character of its demand for total and immediate withdrawal of the U.S. from all south-east Asia with no conditions.

Such a subjective appeal for an immediate leap to an ideal conclusion is in sharpest contradiction to the theory of dialectics as developed by Marx, Lenin and Mao Tse-tung. MLM theory envisages a stage by stage or quantitative advance toward the qualitative change.

Lenin had struggled with Trotsky over this same principle as it applied to the question of stage-by-stage progress toward a socialist revolution in Russia.[5] Since then, in advanced capitalist countries, the Trotskyites have advanced a two-stage policy, but of a reformist rather than a revolutionary nature. They begin with an anti-monopoly coalition of workers and see this developing through peaceful transition to socialism.[6]

By persisting with unrealistic idealism of this kind, the Trotskyites have always ended up in isolation from the people, and have failed to achieve political power anywhere. After the Fourth International's founding convention in September, 1938, it floundered with little following through depression and war. Khrushchov's denunciation of Stalin in 1956 gave it some hope of revival. By 1963, Trotskyite groups in various countries were ready to proclaim the Fourth's re-emergence as a world organization.

Again, it made little progress. But neo-Trotskyism was able to exert a wider influence, as shown by the development of the New Left. People identified with the New Left usually reject any association with the Fourth, but regularly appear in support of its campaigns and philosophy.

They reflect the individualistic ideology of middle income groups in leading capitalist countries, and especially in the U.S. Consequently, they produce selfish slogans which stress the "rights" of individuals to "do their own thing", usually without regard to the effects on others. When they do grapple with social problems, their efforts to invoke Marxism-Leninism appear as idealistic distortions of dialectical materialism.

The latter requires that theory and action should be based on material conditions - on specific and practical problems imposed by the struggle against capitalism and imperialism. Rejecting this, Trotskyite and New Left specialization in the "all-or-nothing" approach promotes spectacular but unrealistic schemes.

These fantasies may excite the imaginations of the unwary. But they also lead thought and action away from quantitative build-ups of concrete, organized achievements which can culminate in qualitative changes. Furthermore, the "all-or-nothing" demand for instant and total results is correctly appraised by most people as impractical and ridiculous. By thus tending to discredit the revolutionary process, all-or-nothing, ultra-left rhetoric actually helps to preserve the *status quo*.

Because of their subjective, unrealistic approach, Trotskyite organizations invariably lead their members to a political dead end. While MLM parties repeatedly have been able to establish socialist governments, the Trotskyites have never succeeded. And their methods guarantee that success will be equally elusive in future. (The assumption that they have had success in assisting such bodies as the U.S. Central Intelligence Agency will be considered later.)

While the Trotskyites and their sympathizers thus regularly discredit themselves, they continue to reappear in new guises which will serve the needs of their social stratum. For example, as the New Left began to fade in the early 1970's, the Trotskyites maintained their search for acceptance within movements or parties where their "socialist" rhetoric might win support.

THE NDP RELATIONSHIP

In this search, they seem to favour the social democrats. (We might also note that on "The Fifth Estate", a 1974 CBC documentary, former agents told how the CIA has regularly tried to infiltrate and manipulate "reform socialist" parties.)

Where a social democratic party is already prominent and not open to coalition, the Trotskyites try to obtain eligibility in that party by avoiding a formal party structure of their own.

Accordingly, their "Revolutionary Workers' Party" in Canada was abandoned early in the 1960's in favour of a "non-party" League for Socialist Action (LSA). This move enabled them to gain entry into the newly formed New Democratic Party, where their work helped to develop the pseudo-left "Waffle" wing.

But such a "non-party" position does not prevent them from running an occasional candidate. During the Canadian federal election campaign of 1974, an LSA candidate opposed the Liberal cabinet minister, Mitchell Sharp, in Toronto Eglinton. The LSA "non-party" called for "an NDP vote in other ridings across the country."

In Eglinton, according to the LSA's *Labour Challenge,* it was providing a "socialist alternative" to the NDP, which had failed "to propose socialist solutions."

Supporting a "socialist alternative" and non-socialist solutions simultaneously is not surprising conduct from an organization which is both a party and a non-party. Nor is it surprising that such conflicting pursuits should produce some stresses within the organization. The LSA went into the 1974 election in competition with the "Socialist League",a group under Ross Dowson which had "walked out" of the LSA a few months earlier.

While both the SL and the LSA called for the election of an NDP government, they appeared to disagree over tactics. Dowson criticized the nomination of an LSA candidate, and the LSA replied that since the NDP was sure to lose in Eglinton, a "socialist alternative" could safely be put forward there.

Such problems do not arise where no major social democratic party exists. Under those conditions, the Fourth is likely to admit openly that it is a party. Thus in the U.S., Trotskyism is represented by the Socialist Workers' Party (SWP).

A party structure has also been evident in France, where the strength of the Moscow-line Communist Party is such that a similar organization is needed to compete.

But the Fourth's strongest party operations have been in Ceylon (Sri Lanka). Party activities in that country have carried them into a variety of coalitions. Elsewhere, Trotskyism tends to shy away from the strong party concept which is fundamental in the application of MLM theory.

Instead, the Fourth likes to grasp a "host" party, either by coalition or infiltration, with the greatest tenacity. This was shown in 1972 when the Canadian NDP was in the process of purging its Waffle wing. The Trotskyites then regarded their NDP membership as important enough to make it a compulsory requirement for a membership in the LSA. With such a commitment, they were most insistent that some compromise be sought to prevent expulsion of the Waffle.

That campaign was based on "civil rights". Specifically, the Waffle had the "right" to function as an independent group within the NDP. Neo-Trotskyites in the Waffle took the same position. Thus they made it easy for the NDP leadership to attack the Waffle as a "party within the party".

NDP leadership at this time was represented federally by David Lewis, while his son Stephen was at the head of the NDP's Ontario section. Both of these men had won their positions with the support of the Canadian Labour Congress (CLC) which was under some pressure from its U.S. parent, the AFL-CIO, to get rid of the Waffle. The chauvinistic U.S. labour aristocracy could not tolerate the original Waffle demand for independence and socialism.

In yielding to union pressure to oust the Waffle, the Lewises made much of the "party within a party" problem. The most astute Wafflers saw their weakness in that position and tried to shift the battle to the question of NDP subservience to the reactionary AFL-CIO aristocracy. But Trotskyite resistance blocked the move.

As a result, the Waffle as an organization was purged from the Ontario NDP. The Trotskyites took over as the "left" influence in that party. They were tolerated in this because their support for the U.S. union connection meant support for the strength which had backed the Lewises.

The Trotskyites and the Lewises also found common ground in placing the blame for the consequences of foreign investment. David Lewis frequently took the position that he did not blame U.S. corporations for taking advantage of money-making openings in Canada. He blamed Canadians for selling out to them. Similarly, the Trotskyites have concentrated their attacks on Canadian corporations while rarely mentioning any aspect of the U.S. corporate takeover in Canada.

Such basic policy similarities help to explain the Trotskyite connections with the social democrats. The common policy of support for U.S. unions in Canada has nevertheless proved to be unrewarding. The NDP lost 15 of its 31 seats in the 1974 federal election, including that of its leader, David Lewis. The main losses were in labour areas where resistance to U.S. union control was the greatest.

But the semi-alliance between the NDP and the Trotskyites did not end with that election. Further joint action occurred in connection with the overthrow of the leftist Allende regime in Chile by a CIA-supported military coup in September, 1973.

This event greatly disturbed many NDP leaders because it undermined their argument that the grip of monopoly capitalism can be broken by gradualist, parliamentary methods. Allende's type of "constitutional socialism" needed to be propped up.

So when the Peruvian Trotskyite, Hugo Blanco, launched a well-funded tour of Canada late in 1974, the LSA's *Labor Challenge* (December 16, 1974) was able to list supporters from top levels of the NDP. Leaders from some AFL-CIO-CLC unions also indicated support.

Blanco spoke for Trotskyism by rejecting any form of political united front against U.S. imperialism. According to *Labor Challenge,* he "cited as correct" a "massive international campaign" such as that which had won his release from a Peruvian jail. The LSA had been conducting that kind of campaign in denunciation of the Canadian government for delaying the admission of Chilean refugees.

That Trotskyite-NDP policy of concentrating criticism on Canadians rather than on U.S. imperialism is evident in other political and economic areas.

SUPPORTING THE U.S. BUSINESS-GOVERNMENT-UNION ALLIANCE

As double digit inflation extended through 1974, Canadian consumers increasingly directed their anger against U.S. price leaders,who were mainly responsible. In this the consumers were being logical.

They were blaming the main perpetrators of the crime rather than concentrating entirely on the Canadian accomplices.

The U.S. economic system is widely recognized as aggressive and predatory. It should therefore be blamed for the exploitation it commits. As documented in detail by J. K. Galbraith in his *Economics and the Public Purpose* (1973), the U.S. business, government and trade union hierarchies work together to defend and promote their system.

The AFL-CIO worked closely with the Nixon government and with U.S. "multi-national" conglomerates to close down branch plants in support of more jobs for the U.S. AFL-CIO support for the protectionist Burke-Hartke bill in 1972-73 was a major encouragement for that policy.

Subordinate Canadian unions can do little to resist such attempted shifts of employment to the U.S.,because they are outvoted ten to one by their American members and because their union dues are under the control of U.S. headquarters.*

---

*Statistics Canada has calculated from

Far from attacking the subservience of leading CLC unions to the AFL-CIO, the Fourth International has vigorously supported this relationship. The Trotskyite *Labor Challenge* ridiculed the idea that a neo-colonial situation might exist.

> ...what is wrong with Canadian workers' dues going to the U.S.? When the I.W.A. launched an organizing drive in U.S. southern states they used some dues from Canadian woodworkers. That drive organized workers and blocked an employer move to non-union runaway shops. Should Canadian I.W.A. workers object?[7]

The article neglected the obvious answer.

---

returns submitted by U.S. unions that between 1962 and 1972, inclusive, the total income of these unions from their Canadian members' dues and assessments was $155.1 million greater than the amounts returned in salaries, pensions and welfare payments. In 1972 alone, the profit was $26.5 million. (From *Corporation and Labour Union Returns, 1972.*) While striving to have these reports suppressed, AFL-CIO officials have argued that workers get other benefits, but no supporting, audited statements ever appear. The U.S. unions *do* get extra *income* from Canada - from cash deposits and investments totalling $91 million in 1972. Even assuming a return of only eight per cent, that fund would extract another $7.3 million from this country.

Canadian workers should object because the control of their money together with the other constitutional rights often given to the top brass in U.S. unions can provide these officials with dictatorial powers.

A key example of this was the suppression of rank-and-file IBEW workers in 1966 at the U.S.-based Lenkurt (General Telephone and Electronics) plant in Burnaby, B.C. Wildcat walkouts had been protesting the IBEW local's collusion with the company and its failure to stop speedups.

Union officers in the U.S. backed the local president in suspending or expelling the entire office staff of 213, and in placing the local under trusteeship. Militant members were jailed or fined.

This history was reviewed by *Western Voice*[8] as background to a report of new IBEW-employer collusion in April, 1975 at Vancouver's Pacific Center (which includes an IBM tower). The union brass used witch-hunt tactics against rank-and-file militants who led walkouts in protest against improper layoffs.

Evidently, such union leaders would be among the last to support nationalization of U.S. firms such as Lenkurt or IBM. That goal required independence from reactionary U.S. union leadership - a fact which the Trotskyites,who are strong for nationalization, refuse to accept.

Such Trotskyite opinions soon began to affect the Waffle, which had originally emphasized independence as an essential first step toward socialism. Included in that influence was the propaganda of the Revolutionary Marxist Group (RMG), which had been accepted as a "sympathizing organization" by the Tenth World Congress of the Fourth International.

The RMG newspaper, *Old Mole* (March,1974) explicitly denied that Canadian members of international unions were under U.S. control. The issue of Canadian *versus* U.S. unions was "a false debate". Canadian union bureaucrats "are a distinct entity and are not merely compradors or puppets to their American partners."

> Their basis of power and privilege rests in control over Canadian locals. If a little more national autonomy would help to deflect anti-bureaucratic sentiment in the Canadian rank-and-file, thereby making control easier to exercise, then they can be expected to renegotiate with U.S. head offices in order to obtain this advantage.

The fact that negotiations are necessary did not appear to be worthy of consideration by the *Old Mole* commentator. Following the line to be expected from U.S. agents trying to divert attention from U.S. imperialism, he ignored the futility of "autonomy" granted by U.S. officials who retain the ultimate authority.

Even if these officials regularly refrain from exercising their power,the fact that it exists must influence even the day-to-day decisions of the Canadian union branch.

Trotskyism thus tries to lead left-wing political movements away from every specific struggle to break Canada's neo-colonial labour relationships with the U.S. Its references to that problem are usually confined to vague and contradictory generalities, which may be shifted frequently in pursuit of public opinion. (This was a pattern established by Trotsky. See below, p.35.)

Following that precedent, the Dowson group (see above, p.16) began a special effort in 1974 to capitalize on growing Canadian resistance to the U.S. takeover.

The group's newspaper, *Forward* (March, 1975) announced that "only a labor government can wrest Canada free from the octopus arms of American imperialism...." But there was no discussion of how such a government could become effective while the octopus arm of the AFL-CIO retained its grip on Canadian labour.

The Dowson anti-imperialist line was apparently a tactical move, made in recognition of the fact that the anti-nationalist position of the LSA and the RMG was "truly disastrous". (*Forward,* July, 1974.)

CANADA'S COLONIAL STATUS DENIED

What does emerge from the above process is a denial of the fact that Canada's union structure is part of its colonial connections. The Dowson group, like the other Trotskyite sects, refused to recognize that independence for Canadian labour is an essential factor in breaking the U.S. grip. By cutting loose from the AFL-CIO-CLC aristocracy, Canadian workers would weaken it. (See below, pp. 137-38.)

So they would help U.S. workers who also seek to escape the power of that reactionary elite. For Canadian workers, that would be liberation nationalism, which has proved to be essential wherever imperialism has been defeated.

The Trotskyites want to ignore that stage, and hope to leap forward at once to a world union of workers which would transcend national boundaries. Such utopian internationalism is a diversion which must please the two superpowers as they proceed with their attempts to exploit and subvert smaller nations.

Another pro-imperialist tendency of the Trotskyites appeared in their reaction to the rapid inflation which began in 1973. Their publications generally avoided any identification of U.S. "multinational" corporations as price leaders.

Relying on the Trotskyites, a consumer would learn little about the effect of U.S. protectionist policies, which helped to keep American inflation at a lower rate than that of most other countries.

Not much would be learned about the price leadership of U.S. conglomerates such as General Foods, Kraftco and Standard Brands. Farmers would never find out that their major cost increases result from the highly profitable pricing policies of U.S. corporations.[9]

Trotskyites and neo-Trotskyites in Canada concentrate their attacks on national capitalists[10] like Dominion Stores and Weston's. There is no recognition that even those which might be called independent are subservient to U.S. production and pricing. (See below, Chapter 5.)

This anti-national philosophy has also refused to consider any kind of quota system to limit or roll back the growing proportion of U.S. teachers in Canadian secondary education. (The 85% Quota Committee estimated in 1973 that faculty in *English-speaking* post-secondary institutions were already over 50% foreign* - mainly U.S.)[11]

Experience has shown that the steady encroachment of U.S. culture can be reversed only if some *specific* minimum in Canadian educational content and personnel is decided on and pursued. But the Trotskyites and their sympathisers reply that all such nationalism is bad.

They argue instead for ideological rather than national distinctions, noting that some Canadian teachers are reactionary and some Americans are radical. These

---

*The Committee challenged a survey by Statistics Canada which showed that 63.4% of 21,425 full-time teaching staff in our universities and colleges were Canadian in 1971-72. Adjustments for those who would not report their citizenship and for those teaching in French language institutions showed that of 20,287 in English language institutions, only 49.4% were Canadian.

exceptional cases, however, do not alter the general situation. The rising proportion of American teachers in Canada constitutes a spearhead of cultural invasion.

Even the "radicals" among these teachers can represent what Jean Cottam has identified as "branch plant socialism". She noted the development by 1968 of internationalist groups at the University of Toronto. They had been influenced by an influx of professors seeking escape from the U.S. draft and from job shortages.

Such a U.S. radical, as seen by Cottam, "impresses our students with his alleged 'progressivism'" and "normally supports independence movements everywhere with the sole exception of Canada." She agreed with Robin Mathews that the left wing U.S. radical thus "unconsciously becomes 'an agent of U.S. imperialism.'"

> U.S. academic radicalism, by unwittingly indoctrinating our young people with contempt for Canadian values and our quest for independence, as well as by contributing to polarization of our society, will bring us nothing but harm.*

Occasionally, the U.S. academic radical becomes a strong advocate of Canadian independence. Then she or he usually becomes a Canadian citizen and a useful ally in

---

* See *Canadian Universities: American Takeover of the Mind?*, Toronto, Gall Publications, 1974,p.27. (Here "polarization" refers to the division of Canadians be-

the struggle against the U.S. takeover.

Other foreign teachers could work in Canada as visitors, or within a controlled quota of 15% or less.(That allowance would be far more generous than in any other country which is not a dependency.)[12]

The Fourth International's refusal to oppose the U.S. cultural, industrial and trade union invasion of Canada shows every sign of being deliberately planned. It raises some questions concerning Trotskyism's possible role as a U.S. agency.

In that role, the promotion of all-or-nothing idealism in left wing ranks would seem to be an obvious approach. Thus we often meet idealist attacks on nationalism in general, with no distinction between the chauvinistic, aggressive nationalism of the U.S.,and the liberation nationalism of its victims.

Canadians who resist the U.S. takeover may even be called "racist". This economic

---

tween those seeking independence and those attracted by U.S."internationalism".

Jean Cottam was graduated with a Ph.D. from Toronto in 1971, and was denied a position at Atkinson College's History Department. She quoted novelist Hugh MacLennan's comment in that connection. "Your story is another sample of a scandalous situation, dangerous to the country's future and present.... How typical that the man who got the job you should have had came out of Wisconsin.... Their graduate school is a factory." (*Ibid.*, p. 30.)

takeover is more subtle than a military invasion, but the objective is similar. The "racist" accusation is no more valid against Canadians than it would have been against the Vietnamese and Cambodians who resisted U.S. military penetration.

While opposing liberation nationalism, the Trotskyites have shown remarkable restraint with respect to the Nixon type of nationalism as revealed by the Watergate affair. This case, according to the U.S. "Socialist Workers' Party" did not represent "an immediate threat to democracy", and was primarily a defense of "national security."[13]

The same kind of sympathy with U.S. ruling class views is shown in Trotskyism's hostility toward countries where socialist revolution has succeeded. These include China, North Korea and Albania. (See below, Chapter 6.)And even after complete success for the liberation fronts in Indo-China, *Labor Challenge* continued to vilify the 1973 ceasefire agreements.

In its view, "only when the liberation forces broke from the framework of the accords" was "the way opened for victory."[14]

This neglected the importance of the political and military preparations made possible for the liberation forces during the two years after U.S. withdrawal. But while avoiding comment on these successful popular front tactics, the writer did warn against "political compromise by the liberation forces' leadership" which might "maintain capitalism in Indochina."

Instant all-or-nothing socialism, an instant all-or-nothing military showdown in 1973 - these were the Trotskyite stratagems for Indo-China. They would have resulted in the same disasters and defeats which have followed them everywhere.

The basis for these positions appears in the record of Trotsky, and in the works of his supporters. The latter include Isaac Deutscher. He wrote voluminously in favour of Trotsky, but in the process he revealed some of Trotsky's weaknesses.

Deutscher's death in 1967 left Ernest Mandel, a world leader of the Fourth International,[15] as the major spokesman for Trotskyism. The persistence of that doctrine and its consequences indicate the need for a better understanding of its background and character.

CHAPTER ONE - NOTES

1 See glossary, "Communist International".

2 From "Behind Today's Trotskyism", *Guardian*, New York, March 28, 1973. This was later included in a pamphlet, *Left in Form, Right in Essence*, by Carl Davidson.

3 *The Militant*, November 10, 1972.

4 *Guardian*, New York, May 2, 1973.

5 See the ensuing discussion of Trotsky's "permanent revolution"; and Davidson, *op.cit.*

6 See the discussion below concerning the approach of Ernest Mandel. See also, Carl Davidson, "SWP's 2-stage Road to Reform",

Guardian, June 13, 1973.

7 *Labor Challenge*, April 10, 1972.

8 *Western Voice*, May 28-June 10, 1975.

9 See "Continentalism and Canadian Agriculture" in G. Teeple, ed., *Capitalism and the National Question in Canada*, Toronto, University of Toronto Press, 1972.

10 See for example, *Last Post*, July, 1973. Typically, when including an American firm such as Safeway, this journal gave no indication of its national origin,nor of its leadership position in food retailing.

11 *New Canada*, July-August, 1973.

12 The 85% Quota Campaign, "Canada Must Have Canadian Universities", Toronto, 1970.

13 Reported by C. Davidson, *Guardian*, February 10, 1974.

14 *Labor Challenge*, May 5, 1975.

15 Mandel's first major action was participation in the abortive French "revolution" of May, 1968,along with Pierre Frank and Livio Maitan. These three constituted the "unified secretariat"of the Fourth International. See Patrick Seale and Maureen McConville, *French Revolution 1968*,London, Heinemann, 1968, p. 52.See also below, pp. 135-37.

Chapter II

THE CHARACTER OF TROTSKYISM

SUMMARY

The Fourth International is called Trotskyite* because its supporters admire and emulate the ideas of Trotsky. They do this because they originate mainly from the same social class as he did.

Trotsky came from a landlord family and had the wealth and leisure time to develop a "love for words".From this background he derived some of the perspectives which are characteristic of dominant property-owning classes.

He published long and "learned" treatises directed toward the "intelligentsia" rather than the average worker or farmer. He also loved drama and the theatre.

Like an actor on the stage, he saw people as a vast audience, to be manipulated. He was interested only in issues of great dramatic value.

In this he resembled the various types of anarchists and provocateurs (who often masquerade as supporters of successful revolutionaries.)

These people constantly seek the spotlight by arranging spectacular confrontations with police, by issuing melodramatic

---

* Members of the Fourth prefer to be called Trotsky*ists*.

statements,or by any other means likely to produce headlines and martyrdom. Such also was Trotsky's record.

He shifted his allegiance among a variety of organizations, wherever he could discern a "popular" cause or an effective platform for his oratory. Throughout the years of their association,Lenin regularly denounced Trotsky for opportunism and inconsistency.

Trotsky's erratic ideas led him to his theory of "permanent revolution." This was an argument against attempts to achieve socialist revolution in poor, underdeveloped countries without first having won power in advanced countries.

The latter, according to Trotsky, were the only ones "civilized" enough to understand the complexities of Trotskyism. And without that understanding, a revolution could not succeed.

In rejecting Trotsky's permanent revolution theory, Lenin asked in 1915 why "for ten whole years life has passed by this fine theory?" Life has continued to pass it by.

But while one country after another bypasses Trotskyism on the road to socialism, the Fourth International remains as a hazardous roadblock for others beginning that journey.

MAIN TEXT

FROM A LANDLORD BACKGROUND TO POLITICAL DISTRUST OF THE PEASANTS

Born in 1879, Trotsky was the son of a well-to-do farmer who continued his acquisitions of land until, as related by Deutscher, his holdings "looked more and more like a landlord's estate." The young Bronstein (Trotsky) became interested in the Spentzer publishing business at Odessa, where "he fell ardently in love with words."

This love affair, according to Deutscher, led to an "intoxication with the theatre" which,

> with its limelight, costumes and masks, and with its passions and conflicts, accords well with the adolescence of a man who was to act out his role with an intense sense of the dramatic, and of whose life it might be said that its shape had the power and pattern of classical tragedy.[1]

Individuals from such an environment tend to regard the average citizen as rude and unsophisticated. Hence they will expect to get his political support by stage tactics - by shifting the spotlight from one dramatic incident to another.

Those who have observed the Trotskyites of the present age shifting from one over-dramatized issue to the next will not be surprised by Lenin's review of Trotsky's early vacillations.

> Trotsky was an ardent "Iskraist"in 1901-03....At the end of 1903, Trotsky was an ardent Menshevik,i.e.he deserted from the Iskraists to the Economists.... In 1904-05, he deserted the Mensheviks and began to oscillate, co-operating with Martynov (the Economist) at one moment and proclaiming his incongruously Left "permanent revolution" theory the next. In 1906-07 he declared that he was in agreement with Rosa Luxemburg. In the period of disintegration, after long "non-factional" vacillation, he again went to the Right, and in August, 1912, he entered into a bloc with the Liquidators. Now [May, 1914] he has deserted them again, although *in substance* he reiterates their paltry ideas. (His emphasis.)[2]

Thus Lenin identified nine distinct shifts in Trotsky's search for the spotlight between 1901 and 1914. Throughout, Trotsky was calling for unity and blaming Lenin for factionalism and splitting.Trotsky was regularly challenging key Leninist concepts: a strong revolutionary party, democratic centralism, and the dictatorship of the proletariat.

Iskra (The Spark) was published in exile by the Russian Social-Democratic Workers' Party as part of the anti-czarist struggle. It was distributed illegally in Russia.

It was a project which must have seemed important enough to justify Trotsky's attention when he joined it in 1901. But when Lenin sought to discipline and centralize the *Iskra* board,* Trotsky accused him of building a closed organization of conspirators and of carrying centralism to excess.This made Lenin "a Robespierre".3#

In the vote on this question, Lenin's group became the Bolsheviks (majority), leaving his opponents as the Mensheviks (minority). The latter were closely connected with the Economists, an opportunist organization which concentrated on economic demands while neglecting political action.

Defeated on the *Iskra* vote, the Mensheviks were brought back to participation in the paper's controlling committee late in 1903 by George Plekhanov. As Lenin's superior in the RSDWP, Plekhanov was making a conciliatory gesture.

In protest, Lenin resigned, leaving *Iskra* to the Mensheviks and the Trotskyites. Trotsky was an eager participant. As we have seen, he was in that category of

---

*Those supporting Lenin were known as the "hard" Iskraists as opposed to the "soft". Lenin also described it as the consistent against the inconsistent, and the workers against the "chatterboxes".4

#Robespierre was a leading tyrant of the French Revolution. He led the "Reign of Terror".

intellectuals whom Mao Tse-tung later described as being interested only in doing big things.[5]

Trotsky's contributions to *Iskra*, however, soon came under attack from Plekhanov because of their "florid rhetoric".[6] (The same tendency toward extravagant style and an unlimited flow of words will be evident to anyone familiar with recent Trotskyism.)

As indicated by Lenin's summary of Trotsky's oscillations, the latter wavered between support for the Economists and Mensheviks on one hand, and his own theory of "permanent revolution" on the other. That theory in itself was a significant digression from the concept developed by Marx.[7] As reviewed by Stalin:

> Marx did not at all propose *to begin* the revolution in the Germany of the fifties with the immediate establishment of proletarian power - *contrary* to the plans of our Russian "permanentists".Marx proposed only that the revolution be *crowned* with the establishment of proletarian state power, by hurling, step by step, one section of the bourgeoisie after another from the heights of power,in order, after the attainment of power by the proletariat, to kindle the fire of revolution in every country....[8] (His emphasis.)

By proposing to begin at once with an all-or-nothing transfer of power to the proletariat, the Trotskyites were neglecting the actual conditions of rural serfdom in Russia. Thus, said Stalin, they "were leaving out of account so important a force as the Russian peasantry, failing to understand that such a policy could only retard the winning of the peasantry over to the side of the proletariat."*

> Consequently, Lenin fought the adherents of "permanent revolution" not over the question of uninterruptedness, for Lenin himself maintained the point of view of uninterrupted revolution, but because they underestimated the role of the peasantry, which is an enormous reserve of the proletariat....[9]

That approach of Lenin's was supported by the experience of the Chinese revolution. From the perspective of Mao Tse-tung:

> The democratic revolution will undergo several stages of development....It is a long process of struggle for the hegemony of the proletariat,a process of winning leadership, which depends on the condition that the Communist party raises the level of consciousness and organization of the peasantry and the urban petty bourgeoisie.... We advocate the

---

*For a summary of the historical development of the Marxist-Leninist permanent revolution theory see George Thomson, "Socialism in One Country", *Broadsheet*, London, April-May, 1971.

> theory of the continuous development of revolution, *but not the Trotskyite theory of a permanent revolution*...We stand for the attainment of socialism through all the necessary stages of the democratic republic. We are opposed to tailism, but we are also opposed to adventurism and ultra-revolutionism. It is *a Trotskyite approach, with which we cannot agree, to reject the participation of the bourgeoisie in the revolution* because it can only be temporary and to describe the alliance with the anti-Japanese section of the bourgeoisie...as capitulationism. Such an alliance today is precisely a bridge that has to be crossed on our way to socialism.[10] (Emphasis added.)

TOWARD ALL-OR-NOTHING SOCIALISM LED BY THE "CIVILIZED" NATIONS.

The Trotskyites have continued to maintain their theory of an instantaneous leap to proletarian power, beginning in the advanced countries and making permanent (uninterrupted) progress to take in the others. Trotsky was faced with the fact that the peasants in Russia had given essential support to the revolution. But he denied that this could be repeated.

The Russian peasantry, he declared, "as a whole found it possible once more - and for the last time in history - to act as a revolutionary factor."[11] He was thus ruling out continued support by the peasantry in Russia or in any other revolution.[12]

Since Trotsky's time, the growing list of successful peasant-supported revolutions has shown how misleading his theories were. Writing in 1928,he still could not find a hint of socialism in the Soviet Union.

"Socialism," he declared,"if it is worthy of the name, means human relations without greed, friendship without envy and intrigue, love without base calculation."

That all-or-nothing pronouncement drew an appropriate response from Carl Davidson in his analysis of Trotskyism.

> Proletarian revolutionaries, of course, must never forget the final aims of their movement. But Trotsky's use of these standards to measure the advances of socialism under conditions of class domination and class struggle reduces the role of the Marxist-Leninist vanguard to that of a Sunday-school parson prattling moralistic aphorisms.[13]

In contrast, Lenin's development of Marxist revolutionary theory in *Imperialism, the Highest Stage of Capitalism* has been confirmed. In that work Lenin provided a basis for understanding the operations of contemporary industrial-financial conglomerates.

He saw that these organizations, controlled mainly by the leading imperialist powers,would inflict the greatest exploitation and ever-increasing misery on the underdeveloped areas. From there the most urgent demands for worker-peasant revolution would consequently emerge.

Throughout the revolutionary process in Russia, Lenin continued to hope for concurrent uprisings in Europe. But unlike the Trotskyites, he did not persist with the view that these uprisings were necessary for the success of socialism in Russia.

Instead, he relied on the peasantry as allies of the workers. Their combined strength would make possible a steady drive forward to socialism.

Lenin also resisted Trotsky's idea that socialism would require an advanced industrial base and would be impossible in a backward country such as Russia.That whole debate showed Lenin's application of dialectical materialism in opposition to Trotsky's utopian idealism.

According to Trotsky, even if a backward proletariat like Russia's did seize state power, it could not survive alone.

> In an isolated proletarian dictatorship, the internal and external contradictions grow inevitably together with growing successes. Remaining isolated, the proletarian state must finally become the victim of these contradictions. The way out for it lies only in the victory of the proletariat of the advanced countries. Viewed from this standpoint, national revolution is not a self-sufficient whole; it is only a link in the

> international chain. The international revolution presents a permanent process, in spite of all fleeting rises and falls.[14]

This reference to permanent revolution, led by the advanced countries, was in conflict with Marx's concept of making revolution permanent in the sense of avoiding interruption as it proceeds stage by stage to state power for the proletariat.[15] Progress of revolution to other countries would necessarily be unpredictable.

As to Trotsky's version, we have noted Lenin's comment that it did not coincide with reality.[16] Events have not supported it since Lenin's time. The advanced countries on which Trotsky depended have not helped socialist revolution, but have resisted it with intrigues, coups and open war.[17]

The largest advanced countries with the necessary military capability have engaged in exploitation of the underdeveloped areas.National power has been used to back external private investment. With the profits thus obtained, these countries have been able to maintain a "labour aristocracy"[18] which,as the AFL-CIO has shown,can be as ruthlessly chauvinistic as the employers.

It is beyond belief that conservative, affluent labour leaders of this type would ever lead a proletarian revolution. Even worse,the AFL-CIO hierarchy has been identified with the operations of the U.S.Central Intelligence Agency. As summarized by George Morris, the CIA in 1967 was found to have been feeding funds through the labour union structure to subvert anti-imperialist labour movements abroad.*

> A clear pattern emerges. The AFL-CIO or its affiliates use the score of trade secretariats of the ICFTU, usually its inter-American branches of representatives, as covers for involvement in CIA operations....American financial aid has become more suspect than ever to unions abroad.[19]

The fact that socialist revolutions have succeeded despite such obstacles is support for Lenin's case against Trotsky's permanent revolution theory.

> Uneven economic and political development is an absolute law of capitalism. Hence, the victory of socialism is possible first in several or even in one capitalist country alone.[20]

VACILLATION, DEVIATION AND OPPORTUNISM

As will be seen when we examine the role of Trotskyism in the Russian revolution, Trotsky's theory would have led to the abandonment of that new socialist state.

---

* Morris quoted Drew Pearson's estimate that CIA money channelled to labour organizations was running at "around $100 million a year."

Instead, it has led Trotskyism into political sterility through its continued failure to achieve the predicted results. The theory seems mainly directed toward support of revolutions where they are least likely to succeed.

Why do the Trotskyites persist with rejection of independent socialist revolutions?The reason is deeply rooted in their elitist, exhibitionist character, which results from their middle stratum origin.

Trotsky showed this perspective in the first issue of his journal, *Borba* (No. 1, 1914).

> The pre-revolutionary Social-Democratic Party in our country was a workers' party only in ideas and aims....Actually it was an organization of the Marxist intelligentsia, which led the awakened working class.

Lenin described this as "the old liberal and Liquidationist ditty which is really the prelude to the *repudiation* of the Party." (His emphasis.)He went on to point out how the petty-bourgeois intellectual wing of the Party had actually specialized in leading the Narodniks,* the Economists, the Mensheviks and the Liquidators.[21]

---

*The Narodniks (Populists) sought to organize the peasants under "intellectual" leadership, while neglecting the workers. Basically, they were individualists who attacked the czar's regime with terrorism and assassinations.

This was a further reference to Trotsky's association with the Liquidators in the "August Bloc". The Liquidators wanted to dissolve the Russian Social-Democratic Workers' Party and replace it with what Lenin described as "an amorphous association functioning legally."

They joined with Trotsky in August, 1912 to form a bloc of anti-Bolshevik factions. With this "August Bloc", Trotsky was hoping to build a bandwagon among the various sects left over from the disintegration and degeneration of anti-czarist ranks after the defeat of the 1905 revolution.

Many unstable elements deserted the RSDWP and some became czarist agents. Others tried to find ways to co-exist with the increasingly oppressive environment. Some became critics of Marxism-Leninism and pursued individualist objectives, including abnormal interest in sensual and sexual stimuli.

Similar trends were evident after the world-wide anti-imperialist demonstrations of the 1960's were curbed by strongly entrenched establishments supported by newly developed "riot control" techniques. At that time, as in pre-War I Europe, too much reliance was placed in the leadership of the intellectual stratum, which invariably vacillates from one opportunist cause to another.

People in this stratum are unstable because they face the world without the confidence which comes from disciplined,class conscious organization such as workers develop in their struggle against the private owners of capital. As ambitious individualists, most intellectuals eagerly seek "respectable" and easy solutions for difficult problems.

With equal concern, they avoid the difficult and often dangerous work involved in building effective anti-imperialist forces. Thus they tend to sympathize with Trotskyite opposition to specific,immediate projects, such as the struggle to free Canadian labour unions from U.S. control.

That outlook also leads to support for the Trotskyite theory of permanent revolution. By denying that a neo-colonial country can gain freedom from its oppressors without "the victory of the proletariat of the advanced countries", the Fourth international finds an excuse for perpetual business in "respectable" organizations.

The Trotskyite approach includes the use of all-or-nothing slogans apparently aimed at dramatizing any event with enough political impact. This succeeds in diverting some organizational energy into ineffective floundering and prevents concentration and unity in dealing with the major problems.

To the extent that potentially effective forces are thus misled, the rule of imperialism is prolonged.Recognizing this, leaders of successful socialist revolutions have been obliged to clear away the Trotskyite roadblock before proceeding to victory.

Further study of such experiences is therefore important to those still seeking liberation.

CHAPTER TWO - NOTES

1 Isaac Deutscher, *The Prophet Armed*, London, Oxford University Press, 1954, p. 17.

2 V. I. Lenin, *Against Revisionism*, Moscow, FLPH, 1959, p. 208.

3 Deutscher, *The Prophet Armed*, pp. 80-84.

4 E. H. Carr, *The Bolshevik Revolution*, London, Penguin, 1971, vol. 1, p. 41.

5 *Peking Review*, December 20, 1968.

6 Deutscher, *The Prophet Armed*, p. 63.

7 Marx & Engels, "Address of the Central Committee to the Communist League, *Selected Works*, Moscow, 1958, vol. 1, p. 110.

8 J. V. Stalin, *Foundations of Leninism*, Peking, FLP, 1965, pp. 36-37.

9 *Ibid.*, p. 35.

10 Mao Tse-tung, *Selected Works*, London, Lawrence & Wishart, 1954, vol. 1, pp. 278-79.

11 L. D. Trotsky, *The Russian Revolution*, New York, Doubleday, 1959, p. 243.

12 Deutscher, *The Prophet Armed*, p. 159.

13 "Socialism in One Country", *Guardian*, New York, April 11, 1973.

14 Trotsky, *The Permanent Revolution*, New York, Pioneer, 1931, pp. 22-27.

15 Stalin, *Foundations of Leninism*,pp.36-39.

16 Lenin, *Collected Works*, Moscow, FLPH, 1951, vol. 18, p. 317.

17 See H. E. Bronson, *The Prevention of World War III*, Regina, Prairie Fire Books, 1971, Chs. 4, 5, 7.

18 See Lenin's reference to "this stratum of bourgeoisified workers" in *Imperialism the Highest Stage of Capitalism*, London, Lawrence & Wishart, 1948, p. 16.

19 George Morris, *CIA and American Labour*, New York, International, 1967, p. 155.

20 Lenin, *Selected Works*, New York, International, 1967, vol. 1, P. 671.

21 For a full discussion of "intellectual" leadership and Trotsky's vacillations, see Lenin, *Against Revisionism*, pp. 202-08.

Chapter III

TROTSKY'S MAJOR PROBLEMS

SUMMARY

Even Trotsky's admirers admit that he was defeated in the Soviet Union because he did not communicate well with the workers and peasants, while Stalin did.

Furthermore, Stalin consistently supported Marxism-Leninism, while Trotsky was described by Lenin as having "never yet held a firm opinion on any important question of Marxism." Trotsky would always "desert one side for the other."

He remained unreliable even after he deserted his former friends to join the Bolsheviks at the last minute as they struggled for Soviet power. Assigned to lead the 1918 peace negotiations with Germany at Brest-Litovsk, he played the role of a spotlight-seeking provocateur.

He made grand speeches, defying Germany and admitting Russian weakness. Germany was thus encouraged to overrun much of the Soviet state. Lenin was obliged to accept much harsher peace terms than he originally contemplated.

Later that year, as the Allied powers were forcing Germany toward surrender, they began to land troops in Russia to overthrow the Soviet government. By 1920, the Red Army had repelled the invaders. But in the process, Lenin had to overrule Trotsky, who repeatedly tried to halt Red Army offensives before they had fully attained their objectives.

As the Soviet government struggled to repair the war-torn country, Trotsky tried to mobilize the workers by "militarizing the unions". Lenin rejected this policy as "an out-and-out bureaucratic approach."

Elitism, opportunism and political exhibitionism were thus the main faults which led to Trotsky's rejection by the revolutionary workers and peasants of Russia. His successors, emerging from the same class background, consequently have the same characteristics and produce the same negative results.

MAIN TEXT

TROTSKY COMMUNICATED WITH THE ELITE, STALIN WITH THE "PRIMITIVE" PEOPLE

As a leading spokesman for the anti-Stalin sects after Trotsky's death in 1940, Isaac Deutscher felt obliged to face the question as to why Trotsky failed in his struggle against Stalin.

Deutscher noted that Trotsky came from a landlord family. Stalin's parents were serfs, and that helped to make class hatred "his first nature". According to Deutscher, Stalin was "no orator" nor was he a "brilliant writer". And Trotsky was "a man of letters of highest repute." But Stalin overcame these disadvantages by having "plenty of acumen and common sense."

Deutscher also conceded, without acknowledging the importance of the concession, that Stalin "could lecture coherently on socialism to small circles of workers."[1] That was probably the main reason for his success against Trotsky.

The same point was admitted by Trotsky himself. And in admitting it, he inadvertently revealed his own character and that of his followers. Stalin, he said, was an "oafish provincial" whose every line of writing was marked with "the brand of banality".[2] Stalin's qualities

> were not the qualities of the historic initiator, thinker or orator.... Stalin knew the life of the aboriginal people of the Caucasus intimately - as only a native could. That aboriginality was in his blood. He loved the society of primitive people, found a common language with them, was not afraid they would excel him in anything, and therefore with them behaved in a democratic friendly way. Lenin valued these attributes of Stalin's....[3]

No such communication has ever been achieved by Trotsky or his followers. As Deutscher admitted in describing Trotsky's address to the 12th Congress of the Bolshevik Party in 1923:

> His central idea was, on the whole, beyond the understanding of his audience. The congress was as usual impressed, but

> this time it was impressed by the *elan* of his speech rather than by its content.The few implications of his thought that the mass of the delegates could grasp were such as to arouse apprehension and even suspicion.[4]

Apparently Trotsky did not condescend to communicate with the masses. And his contemptuous reference to the "oafish provincial" who talked with primitive aboriginal people revealed a basic weakness common to all elitists.

That defect shows why the various Trotskyites and Soviet-line revisionists never get around to serving the people. They regard the people with contempt, to be used rather than helped.

HOW TROTSKY'S HEADLINE HUNTING BROUGHT DISASTER

Trotsky's love of the spotlight was another factor which led to his failure as a revolutionary. Until the Bolshevik Party showed that it was going to shake the world, he remained with opposing groups.

When the czar was overthrown in March, 1917, and replaced by the bourgeois Kerensky government, Trotsky was settled in New York as editor of a Russian journal, *Novy Mir*.(Even at that time he was well attuned to the American way of life.) Later, after his expulsion from the Soviet Union, the U.S. news media generally welcomed him as an opponent of Stalin. (See below, Ch. 4.)

In 1917, Trotsky moved to the biggest spotlight by joining the Bolsheviks a few weeks before the October Revolution. Early in 1918, as commissar for foreign affairs, he was sent to represent the Soviet government at the Brest-Litovsk peace negotiations in Germany.

Later that year, as the Red Army faced attacks on all sides by the "Allied" powers, he was made commissar for war. As we have noted, Trotsky could exert great energy in situations which he saw as important enough to be worthy of his talents.

Lenin was seeking all possible support for the revolutionary struggle and seemed to hope that Trotsky could learn from past errors. According to Trotsky, Lenin stated in November, 1917, that after Trotsky had admitted the futility of governing with the Mensheviks and Social-Revolutionaries, "there has been no better Bolshevik."5

There is no record of that statement except the 1932 facsimile published by Trotsky and widely used by his followers. But even if Lenin had made it, two examples of Trotsky's work would soon have changed his mind.

The first was Trotsky's performance at Brest-Litovsk. The peace negotiations began there on December 9, 1917, following an armistice on December 5. All parties in Russia except the Bolsheviks were advocating continued war.

And within the Bolshevik Party, Trotsky and the Left Communists were against any agreement with the enemy. (This was the same approach as that taken by the Fourth International in 1972 with respect to the Vietnamese negotiations.)

Trotsky argued that with continued war, unrest in Austria or Germany would lead to successful revolution there. Lenin was reluctant to risk the survival of the new Soviet state on such a shaky assumption.

He feared that a renewal of hostilities could overwhelm the country's defences, which consisted of nothing but the remnants of the czar's shattered army.

In Deutscher's sympathetic account, Trotsky "treated this danger lightly." He did not want to sign a peace treaty unless Germany actually launched a new offensive. The Bolshevik Central Committee instructed Trotsky's delegation to sign the treaty on the terms proposed by Germany, but Trotsky disobeyed those orders.[6]

He announced a "no war, no peace" policy, and also informed Germany in a dramatic speech that the Russian army was being demobilized. And he refused to endorse the "terms which German and Austro-Hungarian imperialism is writing with the sword on the flesh of living nations." As related in Deutscher's summary of the speech:

> When the echoes of Trotsky's powerful voice died away, no one spoke. The whole conference sat speechless, dumbfounded before the audacity of this *coup de theatre*.[7]

That provocation brought about a collapse of the peace negotiations on February 10, 1918. Still Trotsky treated the matter lightly, dismissing the German warning of military action as "an empty threat". According to Deutscher:

> He underrated his enemy and even refused to listen to his warning. Great artist that he was, he was so wrapped up in himself and in his ideal and so fascinated by the formidable appeal of his own words that he lightly overlooked its deficiencies.[8]

Deutscher was thus outlining an essential feature of Trotsky and Trotskyism. That particular refusal to obey instructions was later described by Soviet historians as "really a policy of provocateurs, skilfully masked by Left phraseology."[9]

The disastrous results to be expected from such adventurism in a critical situation came quickly after Brest-Litovsk. The Germans launched a major offensive.

Trotsky continued to oppose Lenin's demand for immediate renewal of talks. That opposition later brought the following comment on Trotsky from N. K. Krupskaya, Lenin's widow:

> A lover of fine words, who liked to strike an attitude, he thought not so much how to get the Soviet Republic out of the war and give it a respite to recuperate and rally the masses, as to cut a figure....Ilyich called this a lordly, grand seignior pose....

Lenin, she declared,"did not like Trotsky. He was much too bossy."[10*]

In their new offensive, the Germans took Poland, Latvia, Estonia, and the Ukraine. Finally the Soviet government had to accept occupation of those territories and payment of an indemnity to Germany.

Instead of supporting revolution in Germany, Trotsky's actions strengthened the invader's morale.According to Lenin's comment, Trotsky and his ally Bukharin "actually *helped* the German imperialists and *hindered* the growth and development of the revolution in Germany."[11] (His emphasis.)

Trotsky and the Left Communists continued on their disastrous course. They announced that "in the interests of the international revolution we consider it expedient to consent to the possible loss of Soviet power, which has now become purely formal." This extension of the "permanent revolution" theory was branded by Lenin as "strange and monstrous."[12]

MILITARY LEADERSHIP IN THE WRONG DIRECTION

Possible loss of Soviet power became a tangible threat after Germany's defeat. British, French, American and Japanese

---

*After Lenin's death, Krupskaya worked actively with the Central Committee. During that time her appraisals of Trotsky were enlightening, since she was the only person with close knowledge of Lenin's thinking in the year preceding his death.

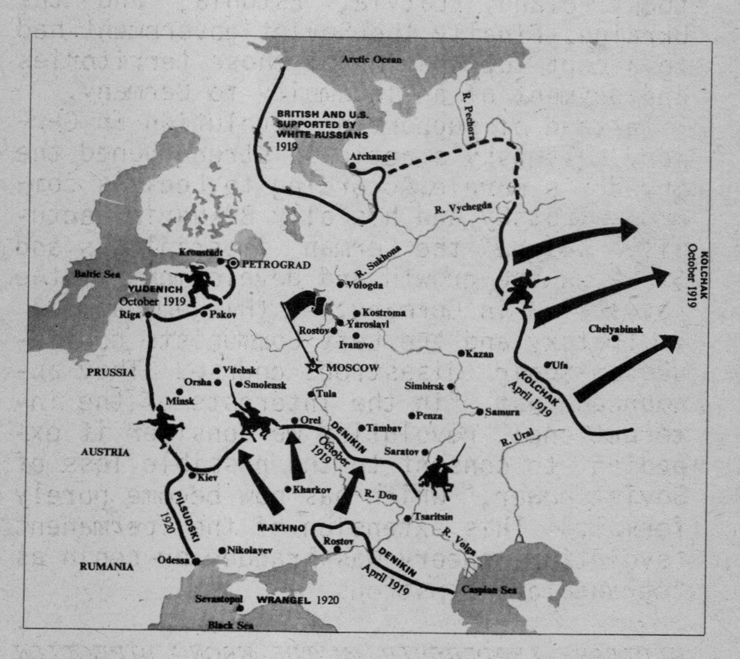

In 1919, "Allied" armies working with White Russian forces under czarist generals and admirals, had surrounded Moscow. To defeat this intervention, the Bolshevik Central Committee repeatedly had to overrule Trotsky's military tactics.

Trotsky speaking in Moscow. He generally failed to communicate with the workers and soldiers, whose experience led them to distrust him. (See pp. 51-52.)

troops attacked Soviet territory without declaration of war. They were supporting White Guard counter-revolutionaries led primarily by Admiral Kolchak and Generals Deniken, Yudenich and Wrangel.

Trotsky argued that the Americans had accepted the Russian Revolution as irreversible "and therefore want to enter into friendly relations with us." He actually asked the American consul to protest the original Anglo-French invasion of August 1918. But by October of that year, U.S. forces had landed at Vladivostok.[13]

Trotsky's friendly contacts with the Americans, which resumed in Petrograd immediately after the revolution, evidently did not discourage U.S. invasion plans. (Here we observe the kind of connection which supports the view that Trotsky had become an American agent.)*

Trotsky's supporters give him credit for the survival and ultimate victory of the re-organized Red Army against the Allied and White Guard invaders. But the Leninists had to overrule Trotsky to ensure that victory.

He had great respect for the "experts" of the old czarist army, together with a contemptuous attitude toward the Red Army cadres. He even ordered some of the latter

---

*According to Carr's investigations, the American military attache, with the consent of his ambassador, "had a long and friendly interview with Trotsky" three weeks after the Soviets took power.[14]

to be shot, and this was prevented only by soldiers' protests and Party intervention.

Early in the war against the interventionists, the eastern front became crucial. The French, British, Japanese and Americans were relying on a huge army led by Admiral Kolchak, who was based in Omsk, Siberia. They proclaimed him "supreme ruler of Russia."

In April, 1919, Kolchak met disaster at the hands of the Red Army and began a general retreat. Then Trotsky put forward a plan calling for an end to the Red Army advance and a transfer of troops to the southern front.

The Central Committee regarded this plan with suspicion, since it would have left Kolchak in possession of the Ural Mountains and Siberia, where the foreign powers could have rebuilt his forces.

The Committee removed Trotsky from all responsibility on the eastern front. Then with the aid of partisans, the Red Army continued its offensive, and completely destroyed the enemy by the end of 1919. Kolchak was captured and shot. A Siberian song summarized the events.

> Uniform British,
> Epaulettes from France,
> Japanese tobacco,
> Kolchak leads the dance.
>
> Uniform in tatters,
> Epaulettes all gone,
> So is the tobacco,
> Kolchak's day is done.[15]

Trotsky's day was on the wane as well. Under his new command in the south, Red Army defeats occurred in battles with Deniken's forces.As the battle neared Moscow, the Central Committee again removed Trotsky, alleging that he had directed the Red Army through regions controlled by hostile Cossacks, where communications were poor.

With Trotsky removed, a revised plan sent the Red Army through territory well equipped with railways, and occupied by a supporting population.[16] As a result, Deniken's armies were broken by decisive actions at Orel and Voronezh.[17]By early 1920 the whole area was cleared and the invaders had to call off their blockade.

They tried once more, however, by organizing a Polish offensive combined with attacks by remnants of Denikin's army under Wrangel. This led to the capture of Kiev,and the Donetz basin was threatened.

Then a Red Army offensive threw the attackers back toward Poland. Trotsky again intervened, as chairman of the Revolutionary Military Council, and ordered the army not to proceed with the capture of Lvov.

He then transferred troops to the northeast, causing a brief but drastic setback before a Polish offensive.[18] Finally the Red Army cleared the Ukraine and trapped Wrangel in the Crimea. There, by November 1920, his army was destroyed.

The main invasion was over, although Japanese activity continued until 1922.But Trotsky's policy of calling off victorious offensives and otherwise disrupting military operations had made the victory more difficult. Contrary to the claims of his supporters, he was more hindrance than help.

Another major difference between Lenin and Trotsky after the revolution involved relations between the Communist Party* and the trade unions. As reported by Deutscher, Trotsky felt that the Party's understanding of the "tasks of the epoch" should be substituted for "the wishes and strivings of the broad social forces which it had led in the revolution."[19]

He felt that the political and cultural level of the masses was too low to justify serious consideration of their views.[20] Thus he arrived at the idea of the "militarization of labour", i.e. the mobilization of workers as in an army. This was needed, in his view, because socialist accumulation would require acceptance of increasing unemployment, the dismissal of redundant workers and a continuous downward trend in wages.[21]

Lenin made the first attack on the militarization proposal in a speech entitled, "The Trade Unions, the Present Situation, and Trotsky's Mistakes"(December 30,1920). In a subsequent pamphlet (January 21,1921) he described Trotsky's policy as "an out-and-out bureaucratic approach."[22]

In their propaganda, Trotsky and his

---

*At the Seventh Party Congress (March 6, 1918) the Bolshevik Party was renamed the Russian Communist Party (Bolshevik).

successors have always specialized in denouncing bureaucracy and promoting "workers' control". In practice Trotsky showed that he favoured control of the workers, by a military bureaucracy.He was overruled by Lenin and Stalin.

Reviewing this controversy, Deutscher noted that when the Party ordered Trotsky to refrain from speaking in public on the trade union question, "Trotsky, unrepentant, sulked."[23] He was still unrepentant, in 1937, as indicated in his "testimony" at a "retrial" by the Dewey Commission in Mexico.[24]

Asked there if bureaucracy was inevitable he replied, "In a poor, backward and isolated workers' state, yes." For democracy, "a more cultivated and civilized country" was required. If Germany could have been brought into a workers' alliance with Russia, the combination "would have given formidable results on the economic and cultural bases of those two countries."[25]

The idea that advanced industrialization makes a country "cultivated and civilized" was certainly demolished when Germany adopted nazism.And we now see China, North Korea,Albania, Viet Nam and Cuba as underdeveloped countries whose workers and peasants have made big gains culturally.

They have virtually eradicated the crime, violence, corruption, prostitution and drug addiction which plague the "advanced, western" countries.

In this argument as in most others,

Trotsky sustained his record of always advocating the wrong course from the viewpoint of the workers. By maintaining that record, Trotskyism has deprived itself of political credibility among all those who have become familiar with it.

To survive, the Fourth International has therefore sought support by denouncing the effective revolutionaries, and by continually attempting more *coups de theatre* in the tradition of Brest-Litovsk.We shall now observe how Trotsky firmly established that pattern during his last two decades.

CHAPTER THREE - NOTES

1 Deutscher, *Stalin*, London, Penguin, 1968, pp. 13, 44-45.

2 Trotsky, *Stalin*, New York,Harper, 1941, pp. 66, 194.

3 *Ibid.*, pp. xv, 258.

4 Deutscher, *The Prophet Unarmed*, London, Oxford University Press, 1959, p. 101.

5 Carr, *The Bolshevik Revolution*, vol. 1, p. 119, ft.

6 Deutscher, *The Prophet Armed*,pp.373-77.

7 *Ibid.*, p. 381.

8 *Ibid.*, p. 382.

9 *History of the Communist Party of the Soviet Union*, Toronto, Progress, 1952, p. 216.

10 N. K. Krupskaya,*Reminiscences of Lenin*,

New York, International,1970, pp.412, 447.

11 Lenin, *Collected Works*,vol.22, p. 307.

12 *History of the CPSU*, p. 218.

13 Carr, *The Bolshevik Revolution*, vol. 3, pp. 96-97.

14 *Ibid.*, pp. 33-34.

15 *History of the CPSU*, pp.236-37, 238-43. See also Carr, *The Bolshevik Revolution*, vol. 1, pp. 356-58.

16 Deutscher conceded Trotsky's "timidity" in failing to pursue Kolchak, but he described the campaign against Denikin as "brilliant in all respects". In his version, the Central Committee had sent the Red Army into hostile territory. But that appraisal conflicts with his admission that the Committee regularly had to correct Trotsky's political errors. (See *Stalin*, p. 216.

17 Krupskaya recalled that after Deniken captured Orel, it was Stalin's plan, approved by Lenin, which rectified the situation. *(Reminiscences of Lenin*, p. 539.)

18 Deutscher approved of Trotsky's strategy, as did Georg von Rauch in *A History of Soviet Russia*, New York, Praeger, fifth ed., 1967, pp. 113, 480. But Praeger has consistently shown an anti-Soviet bias.

20 Carr, *The Interregnum, 1923-14*, London, Pelican, 1969, p. 92.

21 *Ibid.*, p. 93.

22 Lenin, *Selected Works*, vol. 3, pp. 516-48, 820.

23 Deutscher, *The Prophet Armed*, pp. 494-503.

24 This "retrial" was staged by American friends of Trotsky,who felt that he should have a chance to answer the charges on which he was convicted *in absentia* by a Soviet court. See The Dewey Commission, *The Case of Leon Trotsky*, New York, Merit, 1968.

25 *Ibid.*, p. 361.

Chapter IV

WHY TROTSKY WAS EXILED

SUMMARY

When Lenin was dying, Trotsky tried in every way to discredit Stalin's leadership. He also refused to participate in the arduous and detailed work of leading the war-torn country to recovery.

He continued to oppose the recovery program after Lenin's death. This led Krupskaya to sever all connections with Trotsky and his "Opposition" group. Trotsky, she declared, "failed to grasp the democratic principles of socialist construction."

After repeated warnings, Trotsky was banished. He had always been prepared to sacrifice the Soviet state in pursuit of his grandiose but illusory objective, permanent revolution.

He shifted from one country to another, and spent his last three years in Mexico where he was assassinated. During his exile, his exploits and writings were publicized by some leading capitalist journals and by prominent anti-communists.

Trotsky's illusions and his methods have been faithfully perpetuated by his followers. As a result, they have failed consistently to obtain mass support. Like him, their main effect has been to confuse and divide those seeking a more rational and equitable society.

MAIN TEXT

THE FAILURE OF TROTSKY'S GOSSIP CAMPAIGN

In a final attempt to overcome the effects of his prolonged obstructionism, Trotsky took advantage of the illness which practically isolated Lenin during the latter part of 1922 and through 1923.*

Some obstructions in the flow of information to Lenin were admitted by Trotsky himself. He identified Krupskaya as one who "did what she could to protect the sick man from contact with the hostile machinations of the Secretariat."[1]

It seems unlikely that Krupskaya saw her role in that way, although she undoubtedly tried to restrain Lenin from excessive work. But at the time, it appears that Trotsky was supplying much of the information she gave to Lenin concerning the performance of the government under Stalin.[2]

Consequently, anxieties were created in Lenin's mind, leading him to write in his "testament"of December 25, 1922 that "Com-

---

*In an attempt on his life by a "Social Revolutionary" in August, 1918, Lenin had been seriously wounded in the head. He had successive strokes in May and December of 1922 and in March, 1923. After the last seizure he was almost entirely confined to his home. He died on January 21, 1924.

rade Stalin, having become general secretary, has concentrated enormous power in his hands, and I am not sure that he always knows how to use that power with sufficient caution."

> On the other hand, comrade Trotsky...is distinguished not only by his exceptional abilities - personally, he is to be sure the most able man in the present central committee - but also by his too far-reaching self-confidence and a disposition to be too much attracted by the purely administrative side of affairs. These two qualities of the two most able leaders...might, quite innocently lead to a split; if our party does not take measures to prevent it....[3]

It might have been an indication of Lenin's isolation from the government that he believed Trotsky to be preoccupied with administration. As we shall see, Trotsky's disdain for administrative details was a factor in his defeat. Perhaps Lenin was referring to Trotsky's attempts to get his own supporters into key administrative posts, or to his neglect of political factors.

During the last week of December, 1922, the question of Great Russian chauvinism against the minority nationalities had become critical. Stalin described it as "our most dangerous enemy which we must overthrow."(Czarist "Great Russian chauvinism" had been a problem for those non-Russians in the border areas who made up 57 per cent of the total population.)

According to historian E. H. Carr, Stalin was following with "meticulous precision in Lenin's footsteps." He was re-emphasizing Lenin's argument that if they fell into "imperialist attitudes towards oppressed peoples" they would lose the chance of mobilizing Asia against "the international west which defends the capitalist world."

Trotsky totally avoided these discussions on the national question.[4] His position was compared by Lenin to that of Karl Kautsky,a German Social-Democratic leader.

> As for the Kautskyites, they hypocritically recognise self-determination - Trotsky and Martov are going the same way here in Russia. Take Trotsky's articles... and you will find his usual eclecticism; on the one hand, the economy unites nations and, on the other, national oppression divides them....The conclusion is that the prevailing hypocrisy remains unexposed,agitation is dull and does not touch upon what is most important, basic, significant and closely connected with practice - one's attitude to the nation that is oppressed by "one's own" nation.[5]

While ill, Lenin was told that in opposing Great Russian chauvinism, Stalin had behaved with "administrative impulsiveness." But Bukharin admitted that Lenin "had been the victim of one-sided and incorrect information."[6] It led Lenin to dictate a postscript to his testament.

> Stalin is too rude, and this fault, entirely supportable in relations among us communists, becomes insupportable in the office of general secretary. Therefore I propose to the comrades to find a way to remove Stalin from that position....[7]

Was Stalin too rude when he eventually exiled Trotsky from the Soviet Union? A good indication of how Lenin would have judged Stalin under direct observation was provided by Krupskaya.

At a party conference in 1926, she severed connections with Trotsky. Her support went to the Central Committee, mainly on the issue of Trotsky leading an "opposition" against socialism in one country.[8]

If it is true, as the Trotskyites insist, that Lenin received information about Stalin's "bureaucracy" through Krupskaya, her subsequent conclusions are most valuable in appraising the validity of the accusations which brought forth Lenin's testament.

Emphasizing the importance of "socialist revolutionary democratism", she identified this issue as the one which "most divided Lenin and Trotsky persistently. Trotsky failed to grasp the democratic spirit, the democratic principles of socialist construction, the process of reorganizing the entire mode of life of the masses."

AN ALL-OR-NOTHING LUST FOR POWER

Later, Krupskaya endorsed Stalin's 1927 analysis of the civil war. This was another denial of the Fourth International's claim that Trotsky led the Red Armies to victory and that Trotskyism and Bolshevism were identical.[9]

A basic distinction between Trotskyism and Lenin's Bolshevism was conceded by Deutscher. Trotsky, he wrote, was "actuated by a lust for power, and sticking to the maxim 'all-or-nothing', he refused not merely to serve as Lenin's deputy,but even to attend his normal duties."[10]

Carr has reported a strong impression that Trotsky's passivity was due in part to lack of that political sense and acumen which Stalin "possessed in superabundant degree." Trotsky "found more or less plausible reasons to account for his inaction...."[11]

Among those reasons was "a dogged mysterious infection" which originated while Trotsky was duck-shooting in the fall of 1923. The "illness" led him to seek the sunny south, where he was when Lenin died. As reported by Frederick Schuman:

> This authentic genius was already developing neurotic convictions of his own infallibility and paranoid fears that he was a victim of persecution.... `In the bitter winter of 1923-24, Trotsky, in Tiflis when Lenin died, was informed in time to attend his funeral. He went in-

> stead to Sukhum on the Black Sea shore, thereby committing the first of the major political mistakes that finally enabled Stalin (for whom he had all of the conceited intellectual's contempt toward anti-intellectual proletarians and stupid bureaucrats) to outmaneuver him completely and encompass his downfall.[12]

Carr speculated on "possible psychological factors in the malady that condemned Trotsky to inaction, or provided him with a reason for inaction...."[13] But Trotsky could be very active for his own purposes. Together with Zinoviev, he organized the "Opposition"against socialism in one country.

In effect he was calling for liquidation of the Russian Revolution. In 1925 Stalin denounced this liquidationism as showing

> lack of confidence in the international proletarian revolution, lack of confidence in its victory; a sceptical attitude towards the national liberation movement in the colonies and dependent countries...failure to understand the elementary demand of internationalism, by virtue of which the victory of socialism in one country is not an end in itself but a means of developing and supporting the revolution in other countries.[14]

Stalin thus outlined a principle summarized later by Mao Tse-tung, who stated

Trotsky with a group of oppositionists in 1927.

Leading members of the Soviet Central Committee in 1929 shortly after they had exiled Trotsky. (See pp. 73-74.)
L. to R., Molotov, Mikoyan, Stalin, Kamenev, Voroshilov, Kalinin, Budenny.

that "in wars of national liberation, patriotism is applied internationalism."15

The strength of Stalin's position *versus* Trotsky was thus based on the former's continuing close contact with the basic problems of the new society. In that process, Stalin was gaining the confidence of the people.

A Chinese analysis has pointed out that eventually "Stalin departed from dialectical materialism and fell into metaphysics and subjectivism on certain questions and consequently he was sometimes divorced from reality and from the masses." But China refused to accept Khrushchov's denunciation of Stalin.

> Stalin's merits and mistakes are matters of historical, objective reality. A comparison of the two shows that his merits outweigh his faults. He was primarily correct, and his faults were secondary. ... Stalin was the great leader of the dictatorship of the proletariat and the international communist movement over a whole historical era, and greater care should be exercised in evaluating him.

The analysis went on to conclude that Khrushchov's campaign against Stalin "enabled the Trotskyites, who had long been political corpses, to come to life again and clamour for the 'rehabilitation of Trotsky.'"16

China's disdain for those who help Trotskyism was indirectly supported by Ho Chi

Minh when he called on the Viet Nam Worker's Party to clarify its standpoint "on the question of national independence." The party had been weak in this regard because some members had "unprincipledly cooperated with the Trotskyites."[17]

TOWARD A PERMANENT OPPOSITION AGAINST SOVIET SOCIALISM

Such rejection by those fighting for independence has been well deserved by Trotsky and his followers, who have persistently discounted the importance of the struggle against colonialism. Having faith only in the most "advanced" countries, Trotsky was willing to sacrifice the Soviet revolution in Russia.

He saw Stalin and the Central Committee as "creatively impotent,contradictory, unreliable, blind, cowardly, inept." Noting these comments, F. L. Schuman concluded that Trotsky was wrong on all points. "Being wrong, he was never able to forgive Stalin for being right."[18]

In 1924, after Lenin's death, Trotsky demanded Stalin's removal from the post of general secretary - with the position to be filled, of course, by Trotsky. The 748 delegates who considered that proposal at a party congress voted unanimously in opposition to it.

Trotsky made his final effort in 1927. Encouraged by external enemies, particularly in Britain and Germany, he had travelled widely in support of a general uprising.

On November 7, as workers paraded in Moscow, they were showered with Trotskyite leaflets announcing "new leadership". The campaign was swept from the streets by counter-demonstrations.

A similar consensus was expressed in a referendum of all Party members held just before that anniversary. The results were: 724,000 for the Central Committee; 4,000 for the Trotsky-Zinoviev Opposition.[19]

Trotsky's takeover attempt brought his expulsion to the Kazakh Republic. When he continued his campaign from there, the Party banished him from the country, on January 22, 1929.

Trotsky had in fact shown most of the characteristics which he had identified in Stalin. He had revealed himself to be "creatively impotent, contradictory, unreliable, blind, cowardly and inept." He had pursued objectives so remote as to be unattainable, while remaining indifferent to smaller, achievable goals. In this too, he had assigned his own fault to Stalin,whom he once described as "naturally lazy".[20]

As to the grand objective of overthrowing the Soviet government, Trotsky continued to pursue that in exile.Established first in the Turkish island of Prinkipo, near Istanbul,he prepared anti-Soviet manuscripts for which western interests were said to have offered $1 million - before they were destroyed by fire.

In 1933 he moved to France, and in 1935 to Norway. His violations of political neutrality were making him unpopular, especially in Norway, from where he was expelled in 1936. He finally settled in Mexico. In 1938, he was able to bring 21 people together in Paris to found the Fourth International. His assassination occurred in 1940 at his Mexican residence.

While in Mexico, he increased his involvement with the capitalist media, including major U.S. publications such as *Saturday Evening Post*, *Life* and *Time*. In several articles, *Life* praised Trotsky's "sheer mental brilliance", his "ceaseless war against Stalin", and his "anti-Soviet propaganda".[21]

Among other admirers in the U.S. was Whittaker Chambers, an ex-communist noted for his testimony in 1948 accusing Alger Hiss of communist espionage and conspiracy. Chambers, in one of his books, called Trotsky "the brilliant seer".[22] Richard Nixon had worked with Chambers to set the stage for the McCarthy witch hunt era in the U.S. It was Nixon who prosecuted Hiss to a conviction for perjury.

Nixon could have given his highest award for anti-Soviet activity to Moscow's neo-Trotskyite leadership which denounced Stalin in 1956. First Khrushchov and then Brezhnev went far in emulating Trotsky's attempted dictatorship over the trade unions. They both showed his admiration for the "advanced" countries and his disdain for the Third World national liberation movements.(Brezhnev's admiration for western gadgets and luxuries has been especially noted.)[23]

Revisionism and Trotskyism both discount the revolutionary potential in Third World countries. The people there, however, are not going to wait quietly for revolution to succeed in the "advanced" countries.

They have seen that some other Third World countries have had to brush aside the Trotskyite-revisionist superpower approach in order to gain genuine independence. Those experiences should show the need to "exile" all forms of Trotskyism if liberation struggles are to succeed.

CHAPTER FOUR - NOTES

1 *Leon Trotsky on the Suppressed Testament of Lenin*, New York, Pioneer, 1946, p.32.

2 Carr, *The Interregnum*, p. 289.

3 *Loc. cit.*

4 *Ibid.*, pp. 290-91.

5 Lenin, *The Right of Nations to Self-Determination*, Moscow, Progress, 1968, pp. 149-50.

6 Carr, *The Interregnum*, p. 289.

7 *Ibid.*, p. 271.

8 Deutscher, *The Prophet Unarmed*, p. 306.

9 Krupskaya, *Reminiscences of Lenin*, pp. 330-31, 498-99.

10 Deutscher, *The Prophet Unarmed*, p. 115. Bertram D. Wolfe has compared Lenin's and

Trotsky's approaches to "the relation of the particular to the general." Trotsky's emphasis, he wrote, was on "the supremacy of the general over the particular", while Lenin repeatedly insisted that "the truth is always and everywhere concrete." See *Three Who Made a Revolution*, New York, Dial Press, 1948, p. 193.

11 Carr, *The Interregnum*, p. 280.

12 F. L. Schuman, *Russia Since 1917*, New York, A. A. Knopf, 1957, p. 138.

13 Carr, *The Interregnum*, p. 312.

14 Stalin, *Works*, vol. 7, p. 169.

15 *Quotations from Chairman Mao Tse-tung*, Peking ed., p. 176.

16 "On the Question of Stalin", *Peking Review*, September 20, 1963.

17 B. B. Fall, ed., *Ho Chi Minh on Revolution*, New York, Praeger, 1967, p. 191.

18 Schuman, *Russia Since 1917*, p. 142.

19 History of the CP*SU*, p. 285.

20 Trotsky, *Stalin*, p. 206.

21 *Life*, February 22, 1937.

22 Whittaker Chambers, *Odyssey of a Friend*, New York, Putnam, 1969, p. 217.

23 Seen as "wild about gadgets", Brezhnev's list has included a time-locked cigarette case, a video-phone system, matched shotguns, a Cadillac, a Citroen-Maserati, and a Rolls-Royce. (*Time*, March 26, 1973).

Chapter V

TROTSKYISM AND REVISIONISM

SUMMARY

It was after Stalin's death in 1953 that the U.S.S.R. began to shift toward a form of neo-Trotskyism. Che Guevara in his last diary referred to a similar trend when he identified the "stupid anti-Stalinism" of "North American leftist intellectuals", most of whom have Trotskyite tendencies.

Like the official Trotskyites of the Fourth International, the revisionists of Marxism-Leninism in the U.S.S.R.have tried to undermine revolutionary nationalism. In its place they have been promoting the "limited sovereignty" doctrine.

By that, a superpower assumes the right to intervene, with military force if necessary, to control countries within its "sphere of influence". Thus the U.S.S.R. intervened directly in Czechoslovakia, and indirectly in East Pakistan through support for the Indian invasion of December, 1971.

The resulting creation of Bangla Desh was strongly supported by Trotskyites outside the U.S.S.R. Overthrowing governments by external force is consistent with Trotsky's "permanent revolution" theory, which denies that underdeveloped countries can succeed in revolution without support from "advanced" countries.

While opposing nationalist revolution against imperialism, the revisionists and other Trotskyites still advance leftist slogans of a general nature. This is done to maintain some credibility among radical ranks.

They also try to dissipate popular protest against the superpower campaign to divide the world into U.S. and Soviet spheres. Trotskyite leader Ernest Mandel has been especially articulate in rejecting the idea that the U.S. political-military-industrial machine dominates the Western capitalist bloc.

These activities have retarded the process of uniting all who can be united against the two main enemies of peace and justice among nations - the Soviet and U.S. superpowers.

As part of their diversionary activities,the Trotskyite and revisionist groups maintain a strong campaign against China, which is in the forefront of the Third World drive for unity.

MAIN TEXT

TOWARD OPPORTUNISM AND AWAY FROM MLM PRINCIPLES

With Khrushchov's denunciation of Stalin in 1956, the takeover of Soviet power by a neo-capitalist elite class was complete. [1] Millions of the most dedicated Soviet cadres who might have resisted that elite had sacrificed their lives in the war against fascism.

As the first country to succeed with socialist revolution, the Soviet Union had no previous experience on which to build theory against a resurgence of neo-Trotskyite opportunism.

In the Soviet Union and East European countries, excluding Albania, a form of revisionism and opportunism gained ground, based primarily on opposition to Stalin and the Marxist-Leninist dictatorship of the proletariat.* While these Khrushchov-Brezhnev revisionists maintained opposition to Trotskyism in words, they emulated it in deeds.

Elsewhere, the Trotskyites continued to denounce the Soviet Union. Their main objection was to Soviet "de-Stalinization", which, as David Horowitz expressed it, had been "carried out by the Stalinists themselves", thus preventing "a real probing of the Stalin era...."[2]

C. W. Gonick, the editor of *Dimension,* has revealed the Trotskyite objectives in this area. He noted Deutscher's prophesy that "the intelligentsia would lead a complex, sophisticated industrial society to 'democratic reform'...without a 'great upheaval'". Apparently Deutscher wanted a return to liberal democracy in the Soviet

---

*This is another reference to the revisionist argument that their class struggle is over and that the proletarian state can be replaced by a "state of the whole people."

Union.

Gonick remarked that Deutscher either had not heard of political parties representing classes; or if he had heard, he must have wanted a return of the capitalist class with its parties.3

The Trotskyites have been promoting liberalism because they hope that with a multi-party system they will be able to participate in capitalist politics, either within an Opposition, or in a coalition government. What they would do *with* power, which they have never attained, was indicated by Trotsky's proposals for militarizing labour.

In effect, the Soviet revisionist elite has come to exercise that same type of authoritarian control over the workers.

Soviet revisionism has also approached Trotskyism in its refusal to support anti-imperialist nationalism. In line with Trotsky's permanent revolution theory, his successors continue to accept his "law" that the way out for an underdeveloped country "lies only in the victory of the proletariat of the advanced countries."4

The same attitude has appeared in Soviet revisionist pronouncements such as that of Alexander Sobolev in *New Times* (No. 8, 1971).

A complex problem in the Communist movement is presented by nationalism, which feeds partly on the legitimate national interests of the people and is to a large extent an expression of the pressure exerted by national prejudice. Although the growing influence of proletarian internationalism is gradually forcing nationalism to retreat,no little effort and time is still needed for the principles of proletarian internationalism* to become the sole criterion in relations between all the fraternal parties.

That view fits precisely into the Soviet concept of "limited sovereignty" which was used to "justify" the invasion of Czechoslovakia in 1968 and of East Pakistan in 1971. In the latter case, both Trotskyites and revisionists endorsed the creation of Bangla Desh by means of an Indian army invasion.

In opposing what the revisionist *Canadian Tribune* has called "The Dead End of Nationalism"[5] and in accepting "limited sovereignty" as an alternative,the Moscow led neo-Trotskyites began to revise Marxism-Leninism.

Lenin had warned that a big nation "can commit violence and insult an infinite number of times without noticing it." Consequently,"an abstract presentation of the question of nationalism is of no use at all."

---

*Neither the Trotskyite nor the revisionist version of "proletarian internationalism" can be interpreted as operating under the control of a workers' party, but rather under the control of the privileged stratum which is characteristic of both.

> That is why internationalism on the part of the oppressors or "great" nations... must consist not only in the observance of the formal equality of nations but even in an inequality of the oppressor nation...that must make up for the inequality which obtains in actual practice. Anybody who does not understand this has not grasped the real proletarian attitude to the national question, he is still essentially petty bourgeois in his point of view and is, therefore, sure to descend to the bourgeois point of view.[6]

Lenin was most specific in his explanation of the proletarian attitude toward nationalism.

> The bourgeois nationalism of every oppressed nation has a general democratic content which is directed against oppression, and it is this content that we support *unconditionally*.... Inasmuch as the bourgeoisie of the oppressed nation fights the oppressor, we are always, in every case,and more resolutely than anyone else,*in favour*...But inasmuch as the bourgeoisie of the oppressed nation stands for *its own* bourgeois nationalism we are opposed.[7] (His emphasis.)

The Polish Marxist leader, Rosa Luxemburg, was opposed to Lenin's policy of allowing national groups the right to secede from existing state structures, including the "Great Russian" state. She argued that this "right to secede" was a bourgeois concept.

Luxemburg was not supported in this by the Polish Marxists as an organization. Trotsky, however, announced that they were seeking to change in favour of Luxemburg. Lenin replied:

> The obliging Trotsky is more dangerous than an enemy! Trotsky could produce no proof, except "private conversations" (i.e. simply gossip, on which Trotsky always subsists), for classifying the "Polish Marxists" as people devoid of honour and conscience, incapable of respecting even their own convictions and the program of their Party.

He went on to point out that the Polish Marxists had never moved to amend the program concerning the national question.

> Why did Trotsky withhold these facts from the readers of his journal?Only because it pays him to speculate on fomenting differences between the Polish and the Russian opponents of Liquidationism and to deceive the Russian workers on the question of the programme. Trotsky *has never yet held a firm opinion on any important question of Marxism.* He always contrives to worm his way into the cracks of any given difference of opinion, and desert one side for the other.[8] (Emphasis added.)

COMMON EFFORTS TO DIVERT ATTENTION TOWARD "SMALL POWER IMPERIALISM"

Since then, as we have seen, the Trotskyites and the Soviet revisionists have deserted the side of Marxism-Leninism, especially concerning the national question. In their view, Canada is not a colony in need of liberation. It is an imperialist power, or at least a "junior partner" of U.S. imperialism.

That view was re-emphasized by the "non-party" League for Socialist Action in 1974 as its candidates sought municipal seats for Trotskyism in several Canadian cities. LSA candidate Carl Austin in Edmonton published a manifesto which included a demand to "End Canada's Imperialist World Role".

The main "imperialist" activity was the use of Canadian troops in Mid-East and Cyprus forces of the U.N. From that perspective, other small powers included in that peace-keeping,such as Finland and Ireland, would also be imperialist.

Such are the extremes to which Trotskyism will go to divert attention and energy away from the struggle against superpower imperialism.

Supporting the same view, the revisionist *Canadian Tribune* headlined the demands of "Canadian imperialism" for guarantees from Jamaica against losses due to expropriation. The *Tribune* saw those demands as a response to "the Guyanese nationalization of the Canadian-owned multi-million dollar Demerara Bauxite Co., a subsidiary of Alcan...."9*

Concentration of shareholding is decisive in maintaining control of a corporate conglomerate.# And the concentration is usually in the "metropolitan" country rather than in the "hinterland".+ Alcan is an example.

Although it has a "head office" in Montreal, it is in effect a U.S. subsidiary. As analyzed by *New Canada*(December,1972):

> Alcan was set up by the Davis and Mellon families as an ingenious device to circumvent U.S. anti-trust laws. It is a parallel organization to the Aluminum Company of America and is owned by the

---

*The *Tribune* (August 23,1972) also told how "the Canadian-owned Alcan Aluminum.. bleeds Brazil...."

#The reported proportion of shareholding by nationality should also be regarded with caution in view of the frequent purchases by U.S. investors of shares on the Toronto stock market. Such purchases, when identified only by number,would be recorded as Canadian.

+The terms "metropolitan" and "hinterland" are academic euphemisms for "imperialist" and "colony". For an analysis of these relationships under the "Alcoa-Alcan combine" see Norman Girvan, *Foreign Capital and Economic Underdevelopment in Jamaica*, University of the West Indies, Jamaica, 1971, pp. 18-24.

same group of shareholders in which the Mellon-Davis interests predominate.... The bauxite is shipped to Canada to be smelted with our cheap hydro-electric power (Kitimat for instance) and then the aluminum is transported to the U.S. for manufacture into finished goods. Canada is just a second link in the chain of colonial exploitation.

As further proof of that link, it may be noted that in 1951, the U.S. government gave specific financial aid to Alcan for the establishment of mining and processing facilities in Jamaica.[10]

Again, in July, 1973, the U.S. tariff commission brought anti-dumping charges against Alcan for selling aluminum ingots in the U.S. below prices charged "by U.S. competitors".

Alcan blamed "technical factors" for the pricing discrepancies and noted that it had "always held to its established policy of following and not undercutting prices offered by United States producers." The tariff commission was told of a "standing joke" directed to Alcan salesmen, asking, "when are you going to become a leader and not a follower (in prices)?"[11]

The Aluminum Company of America (Alcoa), which had originally complained about the price cutting, refused to press charges. It claimed that Alcoa"is not now being injured, nor is it likely to be injured in the reasonably foreseeable future" by Canadian imports.

Evidently Alcoa, as a U.S. price leader, had made sure that minor transgressions by Alcan would not soon recur.

These circumstances show that Alcan does little to support the revisionist-Trotskyite case for"Canadian imperialism". But for a last defense of that case, its supporters usually depend on Brascan, a Canadian-incorporated holding company, which until 1969 was Brazilian Traction, Light and Power.

As pointed out in a 1973 article, "The Brascan File", in the neo-Trotskyite *Last Post*, Brascan has been diversifying widely with help from the Canadian Export Development Corporation. Its Brazilian subsidiaries include food processing, transportation, hotels, and 83 per cent of the country's major light and power service.*

Last Post made much of the Ottawa government's involvement in making EDC loans to Brascan. It also emphasized that Brascan president J. Moore "is a Liberal Party luminary, and one of the founders and biggest financial backers of the Committee for an Independent Canada."

Other links between Brascan and the Liberals led to the conclusion that the company"fits the current Liberal Party theory of business - the expansion of a vigorous

---

* Brascan's assets in 1974 were recorded at $1.9 billion. Its $119 million net income that year ranked it tenth among "Canadian" corporations, compared to a ranking of fourth in 1971.

Canadian investment policy abroad." The EDC loan was explained by the fact that Brascan"is trying feverishly to diversify, and the current pro-multinational policy of the Liberal government supports the idea of diversification of a Canadian company."*

These remarkable neo-Trotskyite conclusions were put forward without apparent attention to some facts presented sporadically within the same *Last Post* article.

> ...of the few Canadian multinationals of any significance, several - among them Brascan - *are majority owned in the United States*. (Emphasis added.)
>
> In October,1965, the United States Agency for International Development (AID) announced a $40 million loan to Brazilian Traction.
>
> The Science Council of Canada, under Gillespie, "found that Canadian-based multinationals were no more inclined to act in Canadian interests than foreign-based multinationals."
>
> In 1969 the company [Brascan]was averaging an annual withdrawal from Brazil of $17.5 million for dividends *in Canada*,

---

*As further proof of the same process, *Last Post* noted that Alcan had also "managed to pull down $14.7 million in EDC credits since the mid-sixties," and that EDC also insures against risks not normally accepted by private insurance.

> *the U.S. and Europe. At that time they were paying no corporate tax to the Canadian government.* (Emphasis added.)

The fact that the Canadian government and some Canadian capitalists assist U.S.-controlled conglomerates in the extension of their global investments does not make Canada an imperialist power. One might as well argue that the Saigon government, by co-operating with the U.S.,was thereby imperialist; or that Sweden is imperialist because its private entrepreneurs have substantial investments abroad.

The key element in any valid imperialist operation is decisive financial and military strength such as that which the U.S. exerts.By neglecting that fact and by distracting attention to the "imperialism" of small countries, the revisionists and Trotskyites render valuable service to the real imperialists. They violate the most basic rule of guerrilla warfare and political warfare - the concentration of all available forces against the weakest link in the defences of the major enemy.

What they favour is the dispersal of liberation forces against all oppressors, large and small. They also oppose anti-imperialist nationalism, equating it with chauvinistic, superpower nationalism.

A most explicit statement of that opposition was made late in 1974 by a leading spokesman for the Saskatchewan Waffle. He was expressing the dominant view of that organization.

> We must flatfootedly state that the contradiction between capital and labour is the primary contradiction we face... capital is international - it seeks profitable investment locations without regard to political boundaries or national sensibilities...The Canadian bourgeoisie exists - weak and compromised though it may be - and politically our primary struggle is with that class.*

So this "Marxist" analysis identified its major enemy as being "weak and compromised". At the same time it conceded the Canadian economy to be "overwhelmingly American-dominated - to an extent unknown in other advanced countries." But those in the Waffle who proposed to deal first with that overwhelming domination were accused of "going so far as to suggest that the struggle against U.S. imperialism is primary."

Understandably, the members thus accused began to seek more logical political out-

---

*See John Conway, "The Choices Before the Saskatchewan Waffle",Regina, November 1974, mimeo. The Saskatchewan section of the Waffle movement became dominated by U.S. "New Left" ideology, which lacks any real appreciation of colonial struggle and of the need for national independence as a weapon against superpower control. The Saskatchewan Waffle was also influenced by the Revolutionary Marxist Group (RMG), a "sympathizing organization of the Fourth International."

lets. Many of them became familiar with the MLM analysis which concludes that those who reject unity with all possible allies against the main enemy are, in effect, agents of that enemy. They had seen that in Chile, under Allende, the main enemy was the U.S. - as the major supporter and instigator of the fascist coup by the Chilean armed forces in September, 1973. They had seen the disaster that resulted from attempts by Allende and his Communist Party (Moscow-line) allies to collaborate with those armed forces instead of uniting with all possible allies against them.

Conversely, they knew that in Viet Nam, the National Liberation Front had forced the U.S. invaders to withdraw by uniting all possible sectors of the society which favoured independence. And they were learning that in China, a common front against the Japanese invaders had proved to be essential in the final liberation of that country.

Despite such lessons, the Trotskyites within the Waffle developed decisive opposition against united front tactics in the fight against the major class enemy, superpower imperialism. These people apparently came to regard the steady U.S. takeover in Canada as only a minor threat. (Some RMG spokesmen were even heard to say that U.S. imperialism does not exist in Canada.)

Obviously, that line would get full marks from CIA agents seeking to influence left-wing movements in Canada. It would help to shift attention from the strategy outlined years ago by John Foster Dulles, the architect of the Korean war.

> There are two ways of conquering a foreign nation. One is to gain control of its people by force of arms. The other is to gain control of its economy by financial means.

The Trotskyites refuse to admit that the U.S. has the capital to buy out all that remains unsold in Canada. Actually, the U.S. does not even need to use its own capital, since the Canadian banks, trust companies, insurance companies and pension funds are only too eager to supply Canadian savings to help in financing the U.S. takeovers.

Canadian taxpayers' money is often directed toward the same end. In many cases, Canadian federal and provincial governments direct financial aid to help U.S. subsidiaries here. The agency set up to screen foreign takeovers, in its first year,approved over 80% of them as "beneficial" to Canada. Most were by U.S. firms.

Evidently, anti-imperialist nationalism is essential to mobilize Canadians politically and economically to resist and reverse this U.S. encroachment.

In opposing that mobilization, the various brands of Trotskyism may still emerge occasionally with vague anti-imperialist slogans. But these are usually directed toward far-off lands.

They ignore the fact that slogans like "U.S. out of Chile" are ineffectual unless accompanied by tangible action at home. Definite action such as boycotts of U.S. firms and the establishment of strong, independent Canadian trade unions are practical and realistic ways of weakening U.S. imperialism and thereby helping the Third World to escape from neo-colonialism.

When asked to support some definite anti-imperialist action of that nature in their own country, the revisionists, the Trotskyites, and provocateurs such as the "CPC(ML)" all decline to participate. That would be nationalism, which, according to the revisionist *Canadian Tribune*, "screens reformism".12

But the real reformism or opportunism lies with the *Tribune* and others like it. At one time it supported the independent Mine, Mill and Smelter Workers' Union in Canada. Then, in the name of internationalism, it accepted and even defended the union which raided and destroyed Mine-Mill - The United Steelworkers of America.

Also in opportunist ranks despite leftist phraseology, are the neo-Trotskyite Wafflers and some other New Left factions, which prefer to avoid the main enemy in every field. Some such groups in Canada, when denouncing high food prices, concentrate their anger on the Canadian food conglomerate founded by Garfield Weston. When lesser villains are listed, they are also Canadian, or at least are not identified as foreign.

Regularly neglected by these people is the fact that in any Weston supermarket the shelves are loaded with the products of General Foods, Heinz, Campbell, Kraft, Colgate-Palmolive, Quaker, Robin Hood, Proctor and Gamble, Standard Brands, etc. These firms are all U.S.-controlled, and most are identifiable as price leaders. Consistent refusal to mention that fact can hardly be regarded as accidental. We are left then with a deliberate campaign to cover up the role of the American empire in the exploitation of the consumer.

That campaign became more sharply defined as Canadian liberation nationalism grew stronger. The most elaborate attack on that nationalism by early 1975 emerged in *Imperialism and the National Question in Canada,* by Steve Moore and Debi Wells (S. Moore, 70 Beverley St., Toronto).

The arguments of these Trotskyite "Marxist Institute of Toronto" writers are riddled with contradictions and fallacies. (For their total demolition see the review by Jack Scott in *Canadian Revolution,* August-September, 1975.)

To prove that Canada is a "secondary imperialist power", Moore and Wells imply that Canada has a fully independent banking system (p.93). This ignores 1) the well known director interlocks between the U.S. "multinationals" and the major Canadian banks, which consequently supply much of the financing for U.S. takeovers in Canada and the Third World; and 2) the fact that in 1973-74, 170 provincially incorporated foreign banks, mostly U.S., had built up control over assets of $2 billion in Canada. (*Financial Post*, May 3, 1975.)

Moore and Wells also depended on their tabulations showing the government-sponsored growth of "Canadian" multinationals, among which they showed such obvious U.S. appendages as Alcan, International Nickel, and Imasco (p. 24). They were soon refuted by the report that Canada's Foreign Investment Review Agency, in its first year, had allowed 66 of 81 foreign takeover bids on Canadian firms. (*Financial Times*, April 28, 1975.)

Attempting similar proof of Canadian imperialism, the Trotskyite *Labor Challenge* had been tabulating the growing profits of Shell Canada, Gulf Canada, and Imperial Oil. Again, the U.S. connections were ignored. The "analyst",Dennis Marlon, also ignored the use of these branches to build up U.S. "parent" profits.

And Marlon protested a proposed ban on Canadian oil shipments to the U.S. because it would tend "to set American workers against Canadian workers." In other words, resistance to U.S. imperialism should be avoided because it might cause more unemployment there.

Similar strategy was being used by the Communist Party of Canada as it followed the Moscow "detente" line. Its *Canadian Tribune*, in a series denouncing inflationary profits, strictly avoided mentioning the profit figures of U.S. "parent" firms. Instead, it attempted to focus the blame on two small Calgary firms which showed 1974 first quarter gains of $6 million and $4.3 million compared with 1973.

Similarly, the *Tribune* neglected the 50% profit increase of $56 million taken in 1973 by John Deere, the acknowledged U.S. price leader in North American farm machinery manufacturing.* But it reported a 1974 first quarter increase of $2.8 million by Massey-Ferguson,the Canadian price *follower* of John Deere.

After many months of such reporting, the *Tribune* felt obliged to take "a little trip south of the border to pin our prize to the over-stuffed coffers of 853 United States corporations." This belated blanket "award" enabled the donors to avoid specific identification of the key U.S. price leaders.

"Although this is the first time that we have dealt with a 'non-Canadian' company(ies)," the citation read, "everyone knows the effect that these firms have on our lives."#Such are the tactics dictated by "detente".

The assistance thus rendered to imperialism is not a recent phenomenon in the Trotskyite record. Trotskyism was a major source of encouragement to nazi imperialism in its decision to attack Soviet soc-

---

**Special Report on Prices*, Royal Commission on Farm Machinery, (Barber Commission), Ottawa, 1969, p. 72.

#*Canadian Tribune*, June 12, 1974, June 19, 1974, November 6, 1974.

ialism in 1941.

Trotsky had almost invited nazi Germany to attack the Soviet Union by assuring Hitler of victory.

> If the war should remain only a war, the defeat of the Soviet Union would be inevitable. In a technical, economic and military sense, imperialism is incomparably more strong. If it is not paralysed by revolution in the West, imperialism will sweep away the regime which issued from the October Revolution.[13]

While that statement was such as to encourage the nazi attack on the Soviet Union, it could do nothing to ensure the success of that attack. Once again, Trotsky's theories proved to be misleading. But his followers, together with the revisionists, persist in trying to lead the left astray with stories about the incomparable strength of the advanced countries and the futility of anti-imperialist nationalism.

Because chauvinistic nationalism is wrong, they argue, all nationalism is wrong. They accept "national self-determination" as long as it does not involve specific anti-imperialist action or a united front. If the world's exploited people accepted such limitations, they would cut themselves off from attainable victories against the major enemies.

Thus all forms of Trotskyism qualify for the criticism developed from Leninism by Mao Tse-tung.

> Concrete analysis of concrete conditions, Lenin said, is "the most essential thing in Marxism, the living soul of Marxism." Lacking an analytical approach, many of our comrades do not want to go deeply into complex matters, to analyze and study them over and over again, but like to draw simple conclusions which are either absolutely affirmative or absolutely negative....From now on we should remedy this state of affairs.[14]

PROMOTING THE MYTH OF MULTI-NATIONALISM

As a further service to imperialism, the Trotskyites and revisionists scoff at those who denounce attempts by the two superpowers to divide the world between them. Trotskyite leader Ernest Mandel has specifically rejected the "theory of absolute U.S. hegemony" in its sector.

Debating the future of imperialism, Mandel argued that the U.S. could not remain dominant among the non-Soviet capitalistic powers. Like the Soviet economist Y.Varga, he anticipated that European and Japanese capital would break the U.S. grip. Hence, a "huge structural crisis" would radicalize American workers.

He thus neglected the obvious predominance of U.S. financial institutions, which specialize in mobilizing the savings of other countries. The main enemy, in his view, was an anonymous group of "international bankers" working with equally vague "multinational corporations".

This "leading form of organization of monopoly capital today," he declared,"testifies both to stronger international competition and greater international concentration of capital."[15] Against such arguments, two major objections prevail.

1) U.S. firms predominate as providers of the home base for the leading "multinational" conglomerates. In 1973, 10 of the largest 12 MNCs were based in the U.S. These were, in descending order of sales volume: General Motors, Exxon, Ford,Chrysler, General Electric,Texaco, Mobil Oil, IBM, ITT, and Gulf Oil. Of the largest 50, the U.S. accounted for 24, but these took 71% of the total net income.*

2) In crisis, national power is available to exert decisive control over global firms, even if based elsewhere. Thus Nixon's surcharge and devaluation bombshell of August,1971 not only obliged U.S.-based corporations to adjust their international policies. It also exerted severe pressure on other nations,including Japan, Germany,

---

*In this analysis of "global companies" a multinational corporation is one with sales above $100 million, operations in at least six countries, and overseas subsidiaries accounting for at least 20 per cent of its assets. Some 4,000 companies qualify, accounting for 15 per cent of the gross world product.[16]

Italy, Canada, France and Britain.

Similar pressure occurred during the "food and fuel crisis" of 1973, when Nixon restricted soybean exports without warning. This had serious effects on those countries which depended on soybeans for protein, and especially on Japan.

Nixon was in a position to make a unilateral decision in the interests of the U.S. "multinational" corporations which he represented.He acted without warning, and the deprived countries had to accept the decision without being able to retaliate effectively.

In fact the Nixon regime precipitated the 1973 inflation by permitting an unprecedented sale of 715 million bushels of grain to the Soviet Union in 1972. That political decision set the stage for the speculative boom in grain and other foods. A deliberately created oil shortage began a similar speculative price escalation in fuels. The profits of U.S. multinationals soared.

The Soviet people would not have gone hungry without that extra imported food. The luxury-loving elite in that country merely wanted to move nearer the wasteful 2,000 pounds of grain per capita consumed in the U.S. - by converting it mostly into meats.

These selfish actions by the ruling classes in the two superpower nations showed how little they really cared for the people in the hungry Third World. The latter, faced with tripled grain and fuel prices, moved more rapidly toward starvation and economic disaster.

But neither the underdeveloped nations nor the smaller developed powers such as Japan, Britain and Italy were able to avoid the superpower-imposed crisis.

In the final analysis it is nuclear superpower that gives the last word in such conflicts of interest among capitalist nations. Only when the masses of farmers and workers are unified and organized for political and military action does a force emerge which can assert independence from the two superpowers. China, North Korea, Albania, Viet Nam, Laos and Cambodia have shown how that objective can be achieved.

In the meantime, the superpowers seek to recruit smaller countries as allies in their rivalry for world domination. Nixon even urged Japan to take more responsibility for mutual military "defense" in Asia.

These facts reveal the fallacy of the Trotskyite-revisionist"multinational" concept, which has been aptly criticized by Canadian historian Donald Creighton. The multinational corporations,he said, do not serve all countries "with beautiful impartiality...they obey the laws and promote the aims...of the U.S. They are, in fact, imperialist organizations."17

By denying that fact the Trotskyites and revisionists actually assist the superpowers and tend to undermine the national liberation movements, which are essential to the future growth of internationalism.

CHAPTER FIVE - NOTES

1 *Monthly Review*, March, 1969.

2 *Our Generation*, vol. 6, no. 2, p. 17.

3 *Dimension*, vol. 5, no. 6.

4 Trotsky, *The Permanent Revolution*, pp. 22-27.

5 *Canadian Tribune*, March 8, 1972.

6 Lenin, *Selected Works*, vol. 3, p. 749.

7 *Ibid.*,vol. 1, pp. 648-49.

8 *Ibid., pp. 646-47.*

9 *Canadian Tribune*, February 23,1972.

10 Norman Girvan,*Foreign Capital and Economic Underdevelopment in Jamaica*, ISER, Mona, Jamaica, 1971, pp. 21-22.

11 CP, Washington, July 18,1973.

12 *Canadian Tribune*, August 30,1972.

13 R.P.Dutte, *The Internationale*, London, Lawrence & Wishart, 1964, p. 247.

14 *Quotations from Chairman Mao Tse-tung*, p. 215.

15 *New Left Review*,January-February,1970.

16 *Newsweek*, November 20, 1972; *Time*, August 12, 1974.

17 *Financial Post*,August 5, 1972.

Chapter VI

THE RENEGADES IN ACTION

SUMMARY

With his adventurism and exhibitionism at Brest-Litovsk, Trotsky set an example which his successors continue to follow. An important recent case was the Trotskyite collaboration with Soviet propagandists in support of the December,1971 invasion of East Pakistan.

In this they had solid support from the U.S. news media. But none of these crusaders showed interest in freedom for the revolutionary people of *West* Bengal - immediately across the border in India. Instead, they seemed to welcome the attacks by Mrs. Ghandi's army on MLM forces in both West and East Bengal.

When Chou En-lai called for non-intervention by outside powers in East Pakistan neo-Trotskyite journals accused China of "gross and cynical opportunism". A similar denunciation was made when Chou received Nixon at the latter's request, and demanded non-intervention by the U.S. in Indo-China.

Chou guaranteed that China would continue to give full support as requested by the Indo-Chinese patriots, to combat U.S. intervention. The patriots accepted the guarantee as completely satisfactory. But as we have seen, the Trotskyites and revisionists accused China of making unprincipled deals.

They were interpreting China's development of state relations with other countries as the equivalent of political endorsement. Meanwhile they were attempting their own intrusions into China's affairs by promoting candidates to replace Chinese leaders.

They want leaders who will cease the policies of self-reliance and unity which China used successfully against Japanese imperialism and against the U.S. intervention led by Chiang Kai-shek.

In effect, the Trotskyite opposition to the MLM united front against the main enemy serves to support imperialist interests. The same conclusion can be drawn from the opposition to China's Cultural Revolution, which prevented a revival of capitalism in that country.

The Trotskyite, revisionist and ultra-left extremist groups have also ridiculed China's support for the Communist Party of Indonesia (PKI).According to these groups, the success of the CIA-sponsored Indonesian coup showed the inadequacy of united front tactics,and revealed the "pernicious role" played by China in backing the PKI.

Actually, China was refusing to interfere in the PKI's program of support for the Sukarno government. After the 1965 coup, Chinese publications gave prominence to the PKI's self-criticism, and to its recognition of the need for a united front and a people's army led by the working class and not by the bourgeoisie.

Events in these countries have thus helped to highlight the contrasts in policy and philosophy between the Trotskyite-revisionist factions and the MLM parties.

MAIN TEXT

We have seen how Trotsky was prepared to abandon the Russian Revolution after Brest-Litovsk, when socialist revolution had failed in the "advanced" countries of Europe. He was prepared to gamble on continued war as a means of "hastening a European revolution."[1]

The same eagerness for military adventures has been evident ever since among the Trotskyites and revisionists. Their basic goal, despite their Marxist front, appears as a desire to make political gains from the chaos caused by external armed intervention.

APPROVAL OF EXTERNAL INTERVENTION IN PAKISTAN

A major example of this penchant for military adventures appeared in connection with the 1971 upheaval in Pakistan. From the beginning of the unrest there, Soviet and Trotskyite propagandists talked in terms of "liberation" and "self-determination."

This was to be for the people of East Bengal, as part of Pakistan. They ignored the question of liberation for the Indian state of West Bengal - one of the most revolutionary areas in the sub-continent.

A more realistic perspective was offered by *New Canada*, following the Indian invasion of East Pakistan.

> Under the signboard of "national liberation" a reactionary pro-Russian regime has been implanted in East Pakistan.... "Bangladesh means "Bengal nation" in the Bengali language. Calcutta, the largest city in India, is the capital of West Bengal. Does West Bengal not need liberation? Yes, and the people of Pakistan also need liberation.... But it is their task - and one they are entirely capable of.[2]

The article also noted that an immediate action by the Bangla Desh regime under Mujibur Rahman's Awami League was to collect weapons, while a "real people's government *gives* arms to the people."

Because the revolutionaries of West Bengal had repeatedly won a controlling number of seats for MLM candidates in their state assembly, the Indian, Soviet and U.S. governments had a common interest in suppressing them before they made further gains. As Kathleen Gough conceded in *Monthly Review*, the "worst nightmare" for the Indian government was "the liberation of a Red Bengal."[3]

Refugees from East Pakistan, many of whom had been induced to flee by alarmist Indian broadcasts,became an excuse for the invasion ordered by Mrs. Ghandi's government. The Soviet *New Times* agreed with the *New York Times* that the "unprecedented flow of destitute refugees constitutes in effect a bloodless aggression against India."[4] *New Times* moved a step further into fantasy by concluding that the war began when "Pakistan attacked India...."[5]

After the invasion, MLM rebels were disarmed and persecuted in East Bengal until the pro-Moscow *Canadian Tribune* was encouraged to declare that "the Maoists and their extremist Naxalite wing are fragmented and have disappeared as a serious factor...."[6] The Soviet social-imperialists proceeded to proclaim that events in Bangla Desh were "undoubtedly conducive to normalization throughout the Indian sub-continent."[7]

The Fourth International was equally happy with the Bangla Desh developments, at least initially. Like the revisionists, the Fourth's spokesmen described the takeover as "liberation". The main front-page headline on one Trotskyite journal read: "Pakistan Defeat Sets Stage for Bangla Desh Freedom!"[8]

It was almost a month later before the editors reversed themselves and cried, "Hands Off Bangla Desh!" Under Indian occupation, they had discovered, "the Awami League is now trying to firm up a bourgeois regime... India must get out now."[9] They did not say that their own agitation, together with that of the U.S. and Soviet media, had encouraged India's invasion.

Although the Nixon government was supposed to be displeased by India's attack on East Pakistan, the U.S. media consistently portrayed that operation as a fight for "freedom". Rahman's rebels were never described as terrorists - a term always reserved for those who struggle against U.S.interests. "We are grateful to the American press," said Mujibur Rahman.[10]

In view of these circumstances, the New York *Guardian's* assessment of U.S. policy seemed sound.

> The U.S., despite its diplomatic disclaimers, appeared to have accepted the likelihood of a division of Pakistan before the Indian invasion and was already preparing beforehand to advance U.S. economic interests in the divided country. U.S. outrage against India is primarily directed against the extension of Soviet economic and political influence in the subcontinent.[11]

Probably the U.S. position was conveyed to Mrs. Ghandi in her meeting with Nixon a month before the invasion. Those who anticipated mutually beneficial U.S.-Indian arrangements were not surprised when U.S. aid to India and Bangla Desh was renewed just two months after the war.

Nevertheless, corruption, inflation and crime began to move the new nation close to anarchy. By early 1975, the government had declared a state of emergency, and the World Bank was predicting that conditions "can only get worse."[12]

While finding themselves practically in alignment with Soviet and U.S. media concerning Bangla Desh, the Trotskyites were infuriated by China's insistence on non-interference in Pakistan's affairs. The neo-Trotskyite *New Left Review* accused China of "gross and cynical opportunism... that tramples on the cause of proletarian internationalism and deals a heavy blow to the development of world revolution."[13]

That accusation was actually an excellent appraisal of the Trotskyite-revisionist line. A well-known Trotskyite, Tariq Ali, writing in *New Left Review*, anticipated a split in Rahman's Awami League, with young militants moving to "the revolutionary left", i.e., to the Fourth International.

Ali also accused Chou En-lai of defending "the right of the Pakistani army to trample on the aspirations of an oppressed people." This was a reference to a letter written by Chou to the Pakistani government. *New Left Review* reprinted that letter,seeming to confirm Ali's charges.[14]

In fact, the letter emphasized the Pakistani people's right to settle their own problems without external intrusions. Chou made particular reference to the Indian government's "gross interference in the internal affairs of Pakistan by exploiting the internal problems of the country." And further:

The Soviet Union and the United States

> are doing the same...The Chinese government holds that what is happening in Pakistan at present is purely an internal affair of Pakistan, which can only be settled by the Pakistan people themselves and which brooks no foreign interference whatsoever.

It was inevitable that such a declaration would bring forth strong opposition from those dedicated to Trotsky's "permanent revolution", or to the social-imperialist concept of "limited sovereignty". But the foreign intervention led by Soviet-Indian social-imperialism, and supported by the Fourth International proved to be a serious setback rather than a step forward for Bengalese freedom.

In the words of Kathleen Gough, Indian chauvinism in the war resulted in a "massive assault on the Left in West Bengal and other parts of India."[15] She thus implied that the Left in other areas could have advanced the cause of Bengali freedom by rallying support for the MLM principle of non-interference. In both West and East Bengal, the people had shown remarkable ability to organize effectively against their oppressors, including British, U.S. and Soviet imperialism.

UNRELENTING HOSTILITY TO CHINA

Another event which brought forth attacks by Trotskyite-revisionist speakers against MLM principles was the Nixon visit to China in 1972. The Trotskyite Socialist Workers' Party (U.S.) and the Soviet *New Times* both warned against the "deals" being worked out over Indo-China during that visit.[16]

They were trying to label China's program of establishing state relations with all countries as the equivalent of political "deals" and collaboration. While accepting without question the maintenance of diplomatic relations between other countries of opposing ideologies, they were apparently asking China to remain in diplomatic isolation.

(It will be recalled that one of China's main complaints against the Khrushchov revisionist regime was its cancellation of agreements and construction projects in China in an attempt to force political changes on the Chinese. China denounced this action as an extension of political differences to state relations.)

Concerning the Nixon visit to China, J.G. Endicott has shown in his *Canadian Far Eastern News Letter* that China was unyielding on the major political issues. As with Pakistan, Chou En-lai demanded non-interference in other countries' internal affairs. This was clear in his statement to Nixon during the visit.[17]

> We Chinese take the liberty to advise you to go away and leave the peoples of Indo-China to solve their own problems. If you do not, then our position is that we will give the Indo-Chinese people all

> necessary aid, everything they need to achieve their goals of national liberation. We will unswervingly support them to the end.

Chou went on to emphasize that China's position would never change, and that Nixon would have to settle the question of Indo-China with the resistance leaders there.

After the cease-fire had been signed in January, 1973, the Trotskyites and revisionists accused China of avoiding criticism of the U.S. so as not to upset the newly established state relations. In fact, Chinese publications maintained a steady denunciation of U.S. policies.

Referring to the devaluation of the dollar in 1973, *Peking Review* exposed in detail how the U.S. was using this method to "shift the burden of the losses on to the developing countries which have U.S. dollars as their foreign exchange reserves."

Despite these firm Chinese positions,[18] the critics were not satisfied. They seemed to want China to proceed toward armed intervention in South-East Asia. If that brought China under U.S. bombing, the Trotskyites and revisionists could be expected to call on the Chinese people to rebel against their government (as the Trotskyites called on the Soviet people to revolt when nazi invaders threatened Moscow).

In denouncing China's "deals" with the U.S., the Trotskyites were outdone only by similar and even more irrational groups such as the "Canadian Party of Labour" (CPL).*Referring to a number of state visits to China before Nixon's 1972 trip, the CPL declared: "Nixon in Peking will round out a veritable murderers' row of reactionary politicians who in recent months have been filing in to eat at Chou's."

The CPL also derided Chou's methods of persuasion in dealing with extremists during the Cultural Revolution. The CPL journal regretted that the Revolution, which "once almost had Chou En-lai in its grip, has been crushed."

In the CPL view, Chou and Mao Tse-tung "crushed" the Red Guards and other rebels in order "to participate in the capitalist scramble for export markets and trade...." To win trade, "the Chinese economy will be geared more and more to profit-making and the exploitation of cheap labour."[19]

It is not difficult to prove "exploitation" under the Soviet "revision" of socialism. But objective observers agree that China's Cultural Revolution was launched mainly to prevent such revisionism. Since then, the participation of workers in decision-making has greatly increased.[20]

---

* This group, while denouncing the Trotskyite sects, emulates them in its admiration for the AFL-CIO-CLC type of "international unity". (See for example, *The Worker*, May 2, 1975.) This paper praised the "move for international unity" by the United Steelworkers of America, a union aristocracy which is noted in the U.S. for its no-strike deals and company collaboration.

Extremist groups such as the CPL can thus match Trotskyism in wild accusations. But the Trotskyites, while denouncing the Cultural Revolution, saw the Red Guards as allies, not opponents,of Mao Tse-tung. Mao had "hastily called into being" this "new force of an extra-legal character."

> He hurled them against those sections of the party apparatus which he considered to be oppositional and therefore unreliable. Wouldn't it have been more democratic to have first tried to convince the party ranks of the correctness of his ideas?..The fact that Mao decided to go over the head of the party, to appeal to "the masses" against the party is a startling fact....[21]

Little needs to be said in reply to that remarkable collection of inconsistencies.

The Chinese party, with Liu Shao-chi as Vice-Chairman, and also as Chairman of the Republic, had begun to follow the bureaucratic methods prevalent in the Soviet Union. Mao as Party Chairman lacked full control. While the Trotskyites' record indicates that they would not regard Mao's appeal to the masses as democratic, they should not expect the masses to agree.

As the extremist accusations against China reached a new high after the Nixon visit, the New York *Guardian* replied with the conclusion that "The Chinese yielded nothing; the U.S. yielded something." The paper went on to refute Trotskyite attacks by pointing out that the Vietnamese and the Chinese were in full accord.

It appears, however, that these critics of China have dreams which go beyond isolating that country. Each group has plans for revising the government of China itself.

The Soviet Union has been sponsoring Wang Ming, a former member of the CPC Central Committee, as a replacement for Mao Tse-tung.[22] Wang Ming opposed Mao with a disastrous "left opportunist" line between 1931 and 1934. He was sought as an ally by U.S. Intelligence after the Chinese revolution of 1949, but appears to have been recruited first by the Soviet Union.

Trotskyite leadership in China began with CPC General Secretary Chen Tu-hsui, who opposed Mao's united front strategies. Chen's line helped to set up Chiang Kai-shek's slaughter of communists in 1927. He was ousted as General Secretary and was subsequently revealed as a follower of the Trotsky line.

Like Trotsky, he had visualized a long period of bourgeois stabilization in China following Chiang's coup. In fact, there was an immediate renewal of crisis, civil war and peasant revolt.[23]

During the 1966-69 Cultural Revolution, Trotskyites were wondering how anti-government elements might win "a few concessions of a liberalizing nature."[24] Emulating the revisionists, the Trotskyites promoted their own candidate as a replacement for Mao Tse-tung.

This candidate, Peng Shu-tse, announced in 1972 that "the trend in China now is toward political revolution; there is no other way out." He was ready to go back to China "If it was a real revolution...."

TOTAL OPPOSITION TO THE UNITED FRONT

Originally, Peng had opposed Mao's "Stalinist" policy of combining CP forces with those of Chiang Kai-shek to repel the Japanese.[25] Mao,as noted above (pp. 38-39) condemned this Trotskyite opposition to the agrarian revolution and to the united front for national liberation.

Trotsky's position on China, as usual, was in conflict with that of Stalin, who argued that"the more quickly and thoroughly the Chinese peasantry is drawn into the revolution the stronger and more powerful the anti-imperialist front in China will be." Meanwhile, in China, Mao was building that united front against opposition from Trotskyite Chang Kuo-tao.[26]

The incorrect policies imposed on the Chinese CP by Chang Kuo-tao, Chen Tu-hsui and others exposed the Party to the destruction inflicted by Chiang Kai-shek.*

---

* The urban proletariat could lead politically, but was vulnerable to military destruction. Deutscher, in a confused analysis of this period,still seemed partial to Trotsky's argument that Mao's "withdrawal from the cities" could have been a mistake. See *Ironies of History*, New York, Oxford University Press, 1966, p. 101.

Trotsky used that debacle as another argument against the united front.

But Mao succeeded with his efforts to rebuild the front against Japan. The CPC thus created the popular support and the peasant armies which were able to deal with Chiang when he turned on them with American backing after the war.

Despite that success, Trotskyites ever since have continued their all-or-nothing tactics,implying that because a bourgeois-led united front is ineffective, a worker-led front must also be ineffective.

Trotsky pursued that line in the late 1930's with respect to the CPSU's program for a united front against fascism. "There is not and there cannot be a place for it [the Fourth International] in any of the People's Fronts," he asserted.[27]

Extending that idea, the Trotskyites classified the 1965 "Catastrophe in Indonesia" as an example of how all popular fronts must fail. There, the Indonesian CP (PKI) was *following* an anti-imperialist front led by A. Sukarno. His government was taken over by a military coup, which resulted in a mass slaughter of communist sympathisers and a resumption of U.S. investment.

Similar results followed the fascist coup of September, 1973, which overthrew the constitutional government of Chile under "Marxist" Salvador Allende.

The Trotskyite *Labor Challenge* asserted that "Popular Frontism paved the way" for that coup. It ignored the fact that no realistic front should ever include the revisionist CP, which was a dominant element in Allende's Popular Unity government.

The CP actually thwarted the development of a broadly based anti-imperialist united front. As reported in the *Guardian:*

> Right up to the morning when tanks surrounded Santiago, the CP urged the people to "support the patriotic military" and "unite for the constitution and against civil war" - when all along it was clear that the constitution was no more than a scrap of paper to those who were preparing civil war.

Even worse, the CP insisted that the government should enact a gun control law. With that law, the armed forces raided workers' homes to disarm the forces which could have defeated the junta. The revisionist CP showed itself to be a counter-revolutionary instrument of superpower politics.

The Trotskyites argued that if they had achieved a strong organization in Chile, the disaster could have been prevented. The record elsewhere indicates otherwise.

As we have seen, they opposed the National Liberation Front in Viet Nam. That front, they declared, "offers many striking parallels to the tragedy in Spain[29]*(where a bourgeois-led front failed to survive.)

---

*Trotskyite hostility toward the Spanish popular front was one of the demoralizing

The Trotskyites' comparison of Viet Nam's worker-led front with the discredited bourgeois-led fronts in Spain and Indonesia supported Ho Chi Minh's appraisal of them as "agents of fascism".[30] Such agencies would surely try to alienate as many potential allies as possible.*The Fourth's policy in Viet Nam would have provided many more recruits for the U.S.-Saigon dictatorship.

The Fourth had emphasized China's "error" in supporting Sukarno's front. But the Chinese CP was committed firmly to the principle of non-interference in the internal affairs of other countries.

The Chinese did not presume to criticize the PKI or to direct its activities. Instead, they waited for the PKI to revive and do its own criticisms, which were then

---

factors which led to its collapse before effective leadership could emerge. In Canada, the Trotskyite Revolutionary Workers' Party boasted that no Trotskyites could be found fighting in Spain.[28]

*As the Provisional Revolutionary Government began to implement its program for South Viet Nam, it became obvious that they were not making an immediate, idealist leap to pure socialism. With a mixture of private enterprise and socialism, the government was fulfilling its promises to the various classes which had joined the NLF to oppose imperialism. See Wilfred Burchett, "PRG Puts Its Program Into Action", *Guardian*, New York, June 27, 1973.

featured in Chinese publications.[31] As in Pakistan and elsewhere, China had confined herself to supporting the anti-imperialist pronouncements of the Sukarno government.*

The PKI self-criticism noted neglect of the MLM slogan:"Whoever wants to seize and retain power must have a strong army." Obviously, the Indonesian army had not been an instrument of the PKI. Instead, it was willing to sell the country's independence for U.S. dollars.#

Because the PKI had failed to correct that situation, the Trotskyites blamed Mao Tse-tung's foreign policy. It was that policy, they declared, and "above all the disaster resulting from it in Indonesia, that touched off the internal conflict that has shaken China" (i.e. the Cultural Revolution).[32] This concentration of misleading references in one sentence must be a record even for the Fourth International.

The catastrophe in Indonesia resulted from the *neglect*, not the pursuit, of MLM policy. The Cultural Revolution arose, not from foreign disaster but from an internal struggle between MLM forces and Liu

---

*Among other things, Sukarno took Indonesia out of the United Nations in protest against that organization's failure to criticize U.S. military adventures.

#The CIA had made an abortive attempt to overthrow Sukarno in 1958. After the 1965 coup, U.S. banks and industry rushed in at the invitation of the new regime.

Shao-chi's neo-Trotskyite bureaucracy. Liu's elitist organization was beginning to follow the Soviet Union on the road back to capitalism.[33] To blame all that on the failure of a bourgeois-led united front in Indonesia is to forego any claim to credibility.

AGAINST MLM THEORY AND PRACTICE

Such erratic accusations directed against Mao Tse-tung and his foreign policy, and particularly against China's attitude toward the crises in Pakistan, Indonesia and Ceylon, provide clear examples of the Fourth International's opportunism and exhibitionism.Mao frequently commented on the problems created by such conduct.

> What are these people after? They are after fame and position and want to be in the limelight. Whenever they are put in charge of a branch of work, they assert their independence.... It is their dishonesty that causes them to come to grief. I believe we should do things honestly,for without an honest attitude it is absolutely impossible to accomplish anything in this world. Which are the honest people? Marx, Engels, Lenin and Stalin are honest, men of science are honest. Which are the dishonest people? Trotsky, Bukharin, Chen Tu-hsui are extremely dishonest....[34]

The Fourth's dishonest and absurd remark that China had been "shaken" (presumably weakened) by the Cultural Revolution further reduced Trotskyite credibility.[35] China emerged from that revolution with a new dynamism in both domestic and international affairs.

China's renewed vitality also undermined the position of Soviet revisionism -to such an extent that the Brezhnev leadership turned to military threats. The U.S.S.R. built up an army of one million men equipped with nuclear arms on the border with China.

Since the possibility of China invading the U.S.S.R.can hardly be taken seriously, that revisionist army could only be intended for invasion or for intimidation. China's progress, both economically and culturally, has evidently shaken the Soviet revisionists.

The Fourth International has also shown concern about Chinese successes. The campaign to liberate Chinese women must particularly annoy the Trotskyites, who have tried to monopolize that question on a single issue basis, such as abortion on demand, or day care centres. In that process, they have raised "sisterhood" above the class struggle.[36]

But China, and also North Korea and Albania, have made impressive progress in real emancipation of women by concentrating on the class struggle, both internal and external. Women, they say, cannot be fully free and equal until the habits entrenched through many centuries of exploitation have been overcome; or until imperialism and its consequences have been eliminated.

China took an important first step in that direction during the war against Japan. In trying to organize women for the anti-imperialist struggle, they erred at first by denouncing the restrictive activities of the women's in-laws and parents. Renee Blakkan reported the following conclusion:

> The principal contradiction was between Japanese imperialism and the Chinese nation. What we needed was a united front against Japan and instead we were heightening the contradiction between women and their in-laws and parents.

Blakkan has also quoted a Chinese woman as saying that China views the woman question "in the general framework of national liberation and socialist construction."

> The main tasks are fighting, production and education.... To liberate women and improve their education and culture, economic independence should be the point of departure.[37]

The other major questions being faced by socialist countries following MLM principles are also being handled in terms of the class struggle and its extension to national liberation and socialist construction.

The contrast between this approach and the impractical idealism of the Fourth International, or the opportunistic pragmatism of the revisionists is becoming increasingly evident as each new crisis is confronted.

CHAPTER SIX - NOTES

1 Carr, *The Bolshevik Revolution*, vol. 3, p. 46.

2 *New Canada*, March, 1972.

3 *Monthly Review*,March, 1972.

4 *New Times*, no.46, 1971; *New York Times*, October 28, 1971.

5 *New Times*, no. 5, 1972.

6 *Canadian Tribune*, February 10, 1972.

7 *New Times*, no. 4, 1972.

8 *Labour Challenge*, December 6, 1971; December 20, 1971.

9 *Ibid.*, January 17, 1972.

10 *Time*, January 17, 1972.

11 *Guardian*, New York, December 29, 1971.

12 *Globe and Mail*, January 2, 1975.

13 *New Left Review*, July-August, 1971.

14 *Loc. cit.*,

15 *Monthly Review*, March, 1972.

16 *New Times*, nos. 10, 11, 1972, *The Militant*, New York.

17 *C.F.E. Newsletter*, April, 1972.

18 *Peking Review*, May 4, 1973.

19 *Canadian Worker*, August, 1971.

20 William Hinton, *Turning Point in China*, New York, Monthly Review, 1972; Joan Robinson, *The Cultural Revolution in China*, London, Pelican, 1969.

21 *Behind China's "Cultural Revolution"*, New York, Merit, 1967, pp. 49-50.

22 *C.F.E. Newsletter*, April, 1972.

23 *Guardian*, New York, October 25, 1972.

24 *Behind China's "Cultural Revolution"*.

25 *The Militant*, June 30, July 7, 1972.

26 *Guardian*, April 18, April 25, 1973.

27 Trotsky, *The Death Agony of Capitalism*, New York, Pathfinder, 1970, p. 46.

28 *Labour Challenge*, June 5, 1972.

29 *The Tragedy in Indonesia*, New York, Merit, 1966, pp. 5-7.

30 *New Canada*, September, 1970.

31 *Peking Review*, July 14, 1967.

32 *The Tragedy in Indonesia*, pp. 8-9.

33 Bronson, *The Prevention of W.W.III*, ch.X.

34 *Selected Works*, Peking, 1965, vol.3, p.44.

35 *Behind China's "Cultural Revolution"*.

36 *Guardian*, June 6, 1973.

37 *Ibid.*, January 17, 24, 1973.

Chapter VII

AGENTS OF IMPERIALISM?

SUMMARY

Since the beginning of the twentieth century, Trotsky and the Trotskyites have been wrong on every major political issue with which they have been concerned. That is, they have been wrong from the viewpoint of those who seek to end imperialism, neo-colonialism, and wars of aggression.

Conversely, they have been right from the perspective of those who support imperialism and neo-colonialism. Some of these supporters, along with various liberals, also appreciate the Trotskyite promotion of "democratic rights".

One example of how the Fourth International uses its campaign for civil liberties was provided in 1965 when Che Guevara "disappeared". The Fourth took the lead in demanding that Castro should tell what Guevara was doing. When Castro refused, spokesmen for the Fourth concluded that he had either killed or imprisoned Guevara.

The CIA was also hunting Guevara. With help from the Fourth International propaganda and from the revisionist Communist Party of Bolivia, forces led by the CIA found and executed Guevara after he had worked for 11 months with Bolivian guerrillas.

At that time, Castro was also feuding with the Fourth International over its infiltration of the Guatemalan guerrilla movement, MR-13. These guerrillas finally expelled the Trotskyites for "opportunistic and disloyal conduct", including the theft of funds.

The Fourth International again raised a cry about violation of democratic rights, this time by MR-13. Castro pointed out the similarity between the Fourth's propaganda and that of the major U.S. news outlets.

Pro-imperialist activity by the Fourth also became evident in Ceylon, the only place where they have actually achieved a position in government. They had supported a pro-imperialist party, which was defeated by Mrs. Bandaranaike's SLFP in 1970.The anti-imperialist activities of the new government seemed to offend the Trotskyites. Their political faction swung its support to an armed revolt against the government by the petty-bourgeois JVP, which had been unsuccessful in gaining ground with organized labour.

Describing the JVP military assault as a CIA-sponsored coup attempt, Mrs. Bandaranaike's government exerted the force necessary to suppress it. The Fourth sounded a world-wide alarm, labelling the government's action "a violation of democratic rights."

While thus prepared to encourage an armed attack against an anti-imperialist regime, the Fourth also showed an inclination to sidetrack a genuine workers' uprising. The potentially successful worker-student revolt against the French government in May, 1968 was an example.

An overwhelming force of 10 million workers and students dissolved due to lack of leadership and unified objectives. The Fourth, with its world headquarters in Paris, had been promoting "structural reforms", and "duality of power" between workers and capitalists - a line similar to that of the pro-Soviet French CP.

Such education, together with anarchism and the Marcusian cult of spontaneity, was enough to ensure that the marching millions had no clear guidance on how to achieve the power which was within their grasp.

Wherever imperialism is threatened, the Fourth International and its related organizations can be found disrupting, diverting and retarding the revolution.

MAIN TEXT

We have seen how the Fourth International's analysis of Chinese policy has followed the usual pattern of being consistently wrong from the anti-imperialist point of view. It is highly unlikely that anything but a pro-imperialist organization could maintain so continuous a record of misdirection within radical ranks.

ASSISTING THE CIA

A clear case of harmony between Trotskyite and CIA interests occurred in connection with Che Guevara's "disappearance" from Cuba in 1965. Castro had been refusing to disclose Guevara's location, and the imperialist media, supported by the Fourth International, began to accuse Castro of doing away with Guevara.

Eventually the Latin American Bureau of the Fourth claimed to be "convinced that they have assassinated him [Guevara], or that he is incapacitated or confined."[1] Later, of course, events showed that Guevara was leading a guerrilla movement in Bolivia.

By their tactics in this case, the Trotskyites were either trying to undermine Castro,or hasten the discovery of Guevara, or both. The same objectives were high priority for the CIA, which finally helped the Bolivian army to hunt down and kill Guevara in October, 1967.[2]

Meanwhile, the Fourth International had been working within another guerrilla organization - the Guatemalan MR-13. Speaking at the Havana Tricontinental Conference of January, 1966, Fidel Castro drew special attention to Trotskyite infiltration and sabotage of MR-13.He described it as the action of imperialist agents.

Eventually, MR-13 expelled the Fourth for diverting funds and for general misconduct.

> The MR-13 declares before the masses of Guatemala, the Americas and the world, that it is expelling the Trotskyites and

breaking all ties with the Fourth International and all its sections because of the opportunistic and disloyal conduct they displayed within the party and reaffirms its unswerving decision to continue the armed struggle for the program of socialist revolution.

This action led the editors of *Monthly Review* to concede that the Trotskyites suffer from "apparently incurable sectarianism." *Monthly Review* had been criticizing Castro for his "ugly and perhaps ominous" attack on Trotskyism in MR-13, and for his secrecy concerning Guevara.[3] In both cases, events vindicated Castro.

He left no doubt about his opinion of the Fourth's performance. "This position adopted by the Trotskyites," he declared, "is the same as that adopted by all the newspapers and news agencies of Yankee imperialism."[4]

UNDERMINING ANTI-IMPERIALISM IN CEYLON

Castro's assessment was further confirmed as events built up to the armed uprising of 1971 against the government of Ceylon (Sri Lanka). Ceylon is important in the study of Trotskyism because only there has a Trotskyite party ever achieved participation in government.

For Tamara Deutscher, writing in the *New Left Review*, it was "consoling" that Ceylon was "one country in the world, albeit small, where a political party actually gains in popularity by calling itself Trotskyist...."[5]

With their usual policy of shifting alliances, the Trotskyites at one time (1970) had campaigned with the pro-imperialist UNP in Ceylon. (The UNP had formed the government in 1965).

In picking the UNP as a bandwagon to power, the Trotskyites, as usual, were wrong. That party was defeated by Mrs. Sirimavo Bandaranaike's Sri Lanka Freedom Party (SLFP) in 1970. She formed a coalition with the pro-Soviet CP (which had six of 151 seats) and with another Trotskyite faction, the LSSP, which had 19 seats.[6]

Having a big majority within this ruling coalition, Mrs. Bandaranaike was able to move quickly to establish close ties with China. On a state visit to Peking in 1972, she was given firm assurances of support for her policy of independence and neutrality.[7]

Another Trotskyite splinter group, the LSSP (Revolutionary), had broken away from the main LSSP in protest against the coalition. The LSSP(R) then became the official representative of the Fourth International. In that capacity, after the 1970 elections, it denounced the government's anti-imperialist policies as "reformist". Its support went to a new anti-government party, the Janata Vimukhti Peramuna (JVP), which was based primarily on the petty bourgeoisie.

The JVP had limited support among the workers and "ignored the one million plan-tation workers of recent Indian origin." It also failed to project an anti-imperialist program.[8] Instead, in April, 1971, it launched a full-scale armed attack against the Bandaranaike government.

Mrs. Bandaranaike identified the attack as a CIA-sponsored coup attempt. Her forces put down the revolt with losses to the JVP estimated between 1,500 and 10,000 combatants. The Trotskyites denounced this action as "mass slaughter", "unprecedented repression", and "violation of democratic rights."[9]

Two major facts supported the government view that the uprising was instigated by provocateurs with CIA connections. A new constitution was being prepared, abolishing the reactionary Senate and providing for nationalization of private property. Furthermore, the U.S. needed a dependable bastion in Ceylon to counteract Soviet penetration of the Indian ocean.

In a message to Mrs. Bandaranaike, the Chinese government expressed support for her action against the JVP. Jack A. Smith, in an excellent study of China's foreign policy, concluded that China erred in expressing that support, since the Trotskyites were given "an endless supply of mud to cast upon the Chinese revolution."

On the other hand, Smith observed that China could not have supported a revolutionary organization which contained "elements of adventurism and ultra-'leftism' without a mass base, led by a non-Leninist party influenced by Trotskyism." He quoted a Chinese government spokesman as saying that such a movement could not lead the people to revolution and socialism, but "could have resulted in the restoration of a more reactionary ruling group."[10]

Under these circumstances, one could argue that China would have erred by *failing* to express support for Mrs. Bandaranaike's anti-imperialist government.

A most important part of Chou En-lai's message of support was his reference to Mrs. Bandaranaike's concern with CIA involvement in the JVP revolt. "We fully agree," he said, "to the correct position of defending state sovereignty and guarding against foreign interference as referred to by your Excellency."[11]

That such a position should bring Trotskyite mudslinging is understandable. In general, history has shown that the more correct a position is from the viewpoint of liberation forces, the more mud it will receive from the Fourth International. Concern is more appropriate when one's actions receive Trotskyite approval.

Having defied Trotskyism and the JVP, Mrs. Bandaranaike's government proceeded to seek support for a declaration that the Indian Ocean should be a zone of peace. In December, 1972, that declaration was passed by a 72-0 vote in the UN General Assembly, with all the nuclear powers except China as abstainers.

Supporting the declaration, articles began to appear in the Sri Lanka press identifying the two superpowers as the main threats to peace in the Indian Ocean.

These powers, according to one article, were using "visits", "fishing" and "fishery research" to establish a maritime presence and to pursue intelligence operations against the countries in the area.[12]

By supporting armed attack against a government that was organizing against superpower encroachment, the Fourth International showed how the encouragement of provocation and premature revolution might serve imperialism.

SUPPORTING IMPERIALISM WITH DECEPTION AND DELUSION

The Fourth has also shown how to perform the same function by helping to defeat a potentially successful and progressive revolution like the 1968 uprising in France.

The French revolt brought ten million workers and students into the streets against the government of Charles de Gaulle. If properly organized and led, those marchers could have been an irresistible force. Even some sectors of the army and police were regarded as having sympathy for them.[13]

The main organizations which influenced the mass protest were the Moscow-line CP; various anarchist groups such as that led by Daniel Cohn-Bendit; and the Fourth International.

The CP was comfortably established in the French labour bureaucracy, and was aligned with the Soviet policy of avoiding major upsets in U.S.-Soviet arrangements for a division of world power. The anarchists, who worship spontaneity and detest central organization, were accordingly opposed to unified pursuit of state power.

The Fourth International, under the leadership of Ernest Mandel, had its world headquarters in Paris. Just before the uprising, it had reprinted and recommended a pamphlet by Mandel which reflected the organization's approach to political change.

A transfer of power, according to the pamphlet,would begin with"short-term anti-capitalist structural reforms" which would "take away the levers of command in the economy from the financial groups, trusts and monopolies...."

> This would mark the appearance of dual power at the company level and in the whole economy and would rapidly culminate in a duality of political power between the working class and the capitalist rulers.This stage in turn would usher in the conquest of power by the workers.[14]

Evidently this "dual power" approach by the Fourth International was not the one which could have led the French marchers to victory in 1968. It indicated the same passivity and lack of decisiveness which E. H. Carr observed as a basic weakness in Trotsky.[15] These characteristics, together

Barricades burning in Paris during the "Revolution" of 1968 thrilled Trotskyite leader Ernest Mandel, but eventually won votes for the Gaullists.

Trotskyite youth leaders Rudi Dutschke and Alain Krivine in Berlin before the French uprising of May, 1968, which they "led" to defeat.

with opportunism and juvenile adventurism* did much to undermine the French uprising.

Later, Mandel continued to stress "dual power". He advocated a system of workers' councils to provide "the key answer to all the temporary problems of mankind."16

The same diversionary idealism was expressed by Ross Dowson (see Chapter 1). He foresaw "a United States of North America" (U.S.N.A.) being achieved by his version of revolution. It would occur after class struggle had brought strike action "almost to the pitch of General Strikes." He did not say how that pitch would be attained or how his support for the NDP and its AFL-CIO-CLC backers would help.(That U.S. labour aristocracy was already making no-strike deals with the big employers.)

Like other Trotskyite factions,+Dowson's

---

*For example,Mandel "exclaimed joyfully, 'Ah! comme c'est beau! C'est la Revolution!'" when he saw a desolation of burning barricades in Paris streets (including his own car). Every fire was "a vote cast for the Right in the next election." See *Seale* and McConville, *French Revolution, 1968*, pp. 87, 229.

+These include the U.S.-based Spartacist League and the "Bolshevik-Leninist Tendency" (BLT). While agreeing with the mainstream of Trotskyism on North American labour integration, these two "tendencies" otherwise see the Fourth as "reformist". (See *Old Mole*, May, 1975 and *Workers' Vanguard*, New York).

group was neglecting Lenin's warning about imperialism's "labour aristocracy" being "the principal...prop of the bourgeoisie," which would "inevitably, and in no small numbers, stand side by side with the bourgeoisie." (See *Imperialism, the Highest Stage of Capitalism.*)

An NDP government under the influence of the AFL-CIO-CLC aristocracy might be a step toward a U.S.N.A. But one must question Dowson's conclusion that the U.S.N.A. would be socialist and "in no time...would be producing with no other thought than the well-being of mankind."[17]

The well-being of a privileged elite would seem more likely when we consider the wealthy rulers of the AFL-CIO.

Furthermore, Dowson planned to enlist "the aid of highly-skilled technicians" to operate "Canada-wide planning boards". The whole system thus begins to look much like Trotsky's "militarization of labour". It also resembles the Soviet "social capitalism" where "workers' control" means that a managerial stratum gets most of the profit through control of pricing and"bonuses".[18]

Control of "social capital" enables this elite to enrich itself at the expense of workers and consumers.*

---

*Even under U.S. capitalism, some attempts at "workers' control" have begun. For example, a Kaiser steel plant in California was about to close until the owners allowed workers to take responsibility for "making it competitive with Japanese pipe

Despite their record of partiality toward "militarization" of labour, the Trotskyites also seek support with an ultra-democratic, anarchist approach which rejects all central direction - as seen in the French uprising. As part of his struggle against Trotsky, Lenin vigorously denounced both the militarized and the anarchist types of "workers' control".

He emphasized the need of combining democracy and centralism. That approach is standing up to the test of experience as MLM organizations build new societies.

By promoting ineffective forms of "worker's control", Trotskyism and revisionism have demonstrated one more method of misleading and frustrating the forces seeking liberation. They have infiltrated and sabotaged those forces. They have diverted them from the main enemy. They have exposed them by initiating dangerous adventures and provocations. They have hindered them, as in France, by failing to lead when the time was ripe.

They have attacked and distorted the theory developed by Marx, Lenin and Mao Tse-tung, which has provided the analyti-

---

producers." Spurred on by the need to keep their jobs, the workers introduced innovations in tools and methods which raised production 32% in three months, while spoilage dropped from 29% to nine per cent.[20] With "workers' control" they kept their jobs, while Kaiser shareholders got increased profits.

cal framework for every successful anti-imperialist revolution. In sum, they have performed almost every function to be expected of imperialist undercover agents.

GENERAL SUMMARY AND CONCLUSIONS

It is now clear that the political and economic interests for which Trotsky was a spokesman continue to dominate the Fourth International. The pursuit of these interests has led the Fourth into patterns of conduct which are now recognizable.

It seeks to attach itself to any protest movement of the left, using opportunist slogans to mislead, divert and confuse. Wherever imperialism is challenged, Trotskyism will be found undermining that challenge.

Trotskyites encourage susceptible radicals toward premature or misguided revolt as in Ceylon. Or they confuse radical objectives by promoting simultaneous attacks on all enemies, with the result that the main enemy, U.S. or Soviet imperialism, is neglected. This is the Trotskyite "all-or-nothing" idealism, with which they oppose MLM dialectical materialism.

Within the above guidelines, the Trotskyites vary their methods. At times they stress liberal "rights and freedoms", as in their protest against the assumed detention or murder of Che Guevara by Fidel Castro. They will be strong for "national self-determination" when it involves a counter-revolutionary regime such as Mujibur Rahman's in Bangla Desh.

But they resist the kind of nationalism which promotes specific and attainable objectives. Thus they have refused to resist the takeover of Canada by U.S. cartels, labour unions and educational-cultural intrusions. Trotskyites in Canada will call for the U.S. to get out of far-off countries, but never "U.S. out of Canada!" And in Ceylon they obstructed anti-imperialist policies with armed force.

The Fourth favours arbitrary commandism instead of democratic centralism. We have noted examples of this in the attempted militarization of Soviet trade unions, and in the financial sabotage of the Guatemalan guerrilla movement.

In that context, E. H. Carr's comment with respect to Trotsky's trade union policy is still appropriate. With that policy, Trotsky

> had done more than anyone to justify the charge that the dictatorship of the proletariat had been transformed into a dictatorship over the proletariat, and had made it impossible to rally the forces of the proletariat behind him.... It was this paradox which made Trotsky in his new role as the champion of party democracy so vulnerable to the charge of inconsistency.[21]

Inconsistency, then, is a fundamental characteristic of Trotskyism. Its basic inconsistency is the combination of ultra-leftist rhetoric with right-opportunist performance.

Included as other persistent features of Trotsky and his successors are impracticability, aversion to detailed work, and contempt for those lacking a higher education. These features have made Trotskyism a major enemy of the working class, and a favourite of the petty-bourgeoisie.

In those roles, Trotsky committed what Carr has described as six major errors.

1) He failed to state clearly whether he was for or against the party;

2) He elevated himself into a superman, above the party;

3) He opposed the party "bureaucracy" as if work could be carried on without such an apparatus;

4) He set the youth against "the old guard";

5) He emphasized the role of students and intellectuals, thus "depreciating the claims of the workers."

6) He tried "to draw a distinction between groupings and factions and to assert the admissibility of groupings."22

Important additions to that list from the record of his successors are:

1) Opposition to national liberation;

2) Refusal to concentrate on specific struggles against imperialism;

3) Rejection of anti-imperialist united fronts which unite all who can be united for that purpose.

Trotsky and the Fourth International have acted in this manner because they represent the subjective viewpoint of middle income elitists who lack the ability or the will to communicate with working people. They have no real confidence in the workers and farmers. Thus they see no alternative but to seek fame and power by doing "big things", by leaping from one spotlight to another.

Consequently, they are totally unreliable from the workers' viewpoint. As in Ceylon, their lust for power draws them into liaisons with almost any group, recalling Trotsky's flirtations with the Mensheviks, the "Economists", the Liquidators and others.

Being so untrustworthy, Trotsky and his successors have clashed regularly with the disciplined Marxist-Leninist proletarian parties, and frequently have set up organized opposition to these parties. Yet Trotskyite rhetoric always includes insistence on the need for a proletarian party of the purest kind.

Having suffered for decades because of these Trotskyite practices, anti-imperialist forces are ready to repeat and extend the denunciations that began with Lenin. As compiled by F. L. Schuman, Lenin referred to Trotsky as "a poser...a phrase-maker...a Judas...a diplomat of the basest metal...a most despicable careerist and factionalist...the plague of our time."[23]

In Lenin's view, Trotsky's "truly hopeless ideological confusion" made him "more dangerous than an enemy." Since then, MLM critics have concluded that Trotskyism *is* an enemy of the workers - and more dangerous than other enemies in the way that a fifth column is more dangerous than openly opposing forces.

Hopeless ideological confusion is all too common among middle income individualists, including those who seek to find some way to correct the obvious injustices committed by capitalism and imperialism. In this confusion they are accompanied by some members of the working class who have privileged positions, or who are victims of the bourgeois cultural and educational apparatus.

Among these groups there are some who can be attracted by the Fourth International's combination of radical words and opportunist deeds. Others can be driven to irrational extremes because they see their privileges threatened by the effectiveness of MLM anti-imperialism.

These extremists may enrol as imperialist undercover agents. They may join with regular agents and provocateurs to infiltrate radical movements, or to form extremist organizations such as the "Communist Party of Canada (Marxist-Leninist)".

Groups like the CPC(ML) use the familiar tactics of posing as supporters of MLM theory and then trying to discredit it by associating it with wild and irrational demands.* But the effect of such activi-

---

*The CPC(ML) gave an example of this in 1972 by defacing Saskatchewan mail boxes with a poster denouncing the province's

ties is likely to be reduced as genuine anti-imperialists combine MLM theory with accumulating experience.

That combination has led the people of Indo-China to reject the philosophy of the Fourth International and to proceed toward decisive victories against the strongest imperialist power. That struggle will go down indelibly in history as an inspiration and guide to those seeking similar objectives.

China, North Korea and Albania are also developing rapidly on the basis of MLM theory and practice.[24] In the process, they have been obliged to defeat Trotskyism and revisionism most thoroughly before they could advance.

These lessons will not escape the attention of the Third World countries whose struggle for a new world economic order can succeed only when they complete their drive for independence from the "advanced" countries which continue to exploit them.

CHAPTER SEVEN - NOTES

1 *Monthly Review*, April, 1966.

2 R. Scheer, ed., *The Diary of Che Guevara*, New York, Bantam, 1968, pp. 13-15.

3 *Monthly Review*, April, September, 1966.

---

land bank scheme as an imperialist plot. The plan was far from perfect, but it was a step toward social planning of land use and it provided a means of curbing U.S. takeovers of land.

4 *Monthly Review*, April, 1966.

5 *New Left Review*, December, 1970.

6 R. Morrock, *Guardian*, July 18, 1970.

7 *Hsinhua Weekly*, July 6, 1972.

8 *Monthly Review*, January, 1972.

9 *Ibid.*, January, March, 1972.

10 *Guardian*, December 27, 1972.

11 *Ceylon Daily News*, May 27, 1971.

12 *Hsinhua Weekly*, May 21, 1973.

13 *Monthly Review*, *September, 1968*.

14 Ernest Mandel, *An Introduction to Marxist Economic Theory*, New York, 1968, p.78.

15 Carr, *The Interregnum*, p. 279.

16 Mandel, *Revolutionary Strategy in the Imperialist Countries*, Pathfinder, 1970.

17 Dowson, *The Coming Canadian Revolution*.

18 *Monthly Review*, February, 1971.

19 Wheelwright & McFarlane, *The Chinese Road to Socialism*, New York, MR, 1970.

20 *Newsweek*, March 26, 1973.

21 Carr, *The Interregnum*, p. 335.

22 *Ibid.*, pp. 342-43.

23 Schuman, *Russia Since 1917*, p. 33.

24 See Wheelwright & McFarlane, *loc.cit.*; *Monthly Review*, January, 1965, May, 1968, February, 1971, April, October, 1974.

Glossary

BOURGEOIS - Large-scale owners of capital who depend on the exploitation of employees to operate their enterprises at a profit. PETTY-BOURGEOIS - Owners of capital whose labour is supplied mainly by themselves and their families. (May also apply to those with enough income from ownership of stocks, bonds, etc. to affect their social outlook.)

COMMUNIST INTERNATIONAL - The First International began as the International Working Men's Association, which was organized by Karl Marx and his associates in 1864-65. It was dissolved in 1876 after being split and undermined by opportunists and "revisionists" led by Eduard Bernstein.

The Second International, organized in 1889,was a loose association of affiliated European parties and trade unions, with no effective controls. It collapsed as an international entity in 1914 when "revisionists" led by Karl Kautsky of the German Social Democrats broke the International's agreement to refuse support for an imperialist war.

The Third International (1919-43) was seen as an international party, with each national party as a section. Organization was based on democratic centralism, with the central leadership coming from the Soviet Union. The Third International was particularly active in seeking a united front with non-fascist powers against the rising threat of German, Italian and Japanese fascism.

The Fourth International was organized by Trotsky in 1938 to oppose the Third. It lapsed into obscurity during the 1940's after Trotsky's death, but was revived in 1956 following Khrushchov's denunciation of Stalin. The Fourth International formally re-organized in 1963 under the leadership of Ernest Mandel.

DIALECTICAL MATERIALISM - The combination of the dialectical method with materialist philosophy. Dialectics, as developed by Greek philosophers, is a process whereby a thesis and its contradiction, the antithesis, contend until a solution, or synthesis, is found. Hegel, the nineteenth century idealist philosopher, saw history as the reflection of dialectically developed ideas (hence idealism). Karl Marx reversed this, declaring that material things have an independent dialectical development of their own (hence materialism), and thus provide the basis for ideas.

DICTATORSHIP OF THE PROLETARIAT - The use of state power as a dictatorship by the proletariat over the bourgeoisie, with democracy being practiced within the proletarian ranks. This use of state power to suppress the bourgeoisie appears as a reversal of bourgeois state power against the workers while democracy prevails among the property owners. (Bourgeois dictatorship reverts to fascism when seriously threatened.)

ECONOMISM - An opportunist trend which

emerged within the Russian SDWP in its early stages, and which persistently recurs within workers' organizations. It rejects or neglects revolutionary theory and a revolutionary party, while encouraging workers to concentrate on economic gains to the exclusion of political struggles.

IMPERIALISM - "The highest stage of capitalism", according to Lenin's analysis. The most developed capitalist powers, facing a reduction of profits in their highly capitalized economy, turn to the underdeveloped areas to exploit the cheaper labour there. This foreign investment is promoted by means of the financial apparatus with which the industrial and commercial interests have become integrated.

LIBERALISM - While open to a variety of interpretations, the term "liberalism" generally includes emphasis on individual self-interest as the most effective motivating force. That emphasis has led liberalism inevitably to accept the concentrations of wealth and political power resulting from the successes of the strongest, luckiest, or most unscrupulous participants in the struggle for selfish gain. Thus liberalism reveals hypocrisy by professing individual freedom while undermining freedom for the majority who are oppressed by "free enterprise".

LIQUIDATORS - Those among the Menshevik (minority) wing of the Russian Social Democratic Workers' Party who, after the 1905 revolution, demanded the liquidation of that illegal revolutionary party and its replacement by an opportunist organization which would conform to czarist laws.

MLM THEORY - The theory of revolutionary class struggle and of proletarian dictatorship, based on Marx's interpretation of dialectical and historical materialism as developed and applied by Lenin and Mao Tse-tung.

NEO-TROTSKYISM - A New Left tendency to accept the idealist, adventurist and opportunist vacillations of Trotskyism. In many cases these followers of Trotskyite ideology vigorously repudiate the formal political structure of the Fourth International.

NEW LEFT - A political trend which developed out of protest against the Viet Nam war and other imperialist injustices. It has tended mainly to neo-Trotskyism.

PROLETARIAT - Workers without access to capital except by means of selling their labour power to owners of capital.

SOCIAL IMPERIALISM - The combination of socialism in words and imperialism in deeds. The Soviet Union has been described as social-imperialist by MLM critics.

Selected Bibliography

BOOKS

Carr, E.H., *The Bolshevik Revolution*, London, Penguin, 1971, vols. 1-3;*The Interregnum, 1923-24*, London, Pelican, 1969.

Dutte, R.P., *The Internationale*, London, Lawrence & Wishart, 1964.

Deutscher, Isaac, *The Prophet Armed*, London, Oxford University Press, 1954; *The Prophet Unarmed*, London, Oxford University Press, 1959; *Stalin*, London, Penguin, 1968.

Dewey Commission, *The Case of Leon Trotsky*, New York, Merit, 1968.

Fall, B.B. (ed.), *Ho Chi Minh on Revolution*, New York, Praeger, 1967.

Girvan, Norman, *Foreign Capital and Economic Development in Jamaica*, Kingston, Jamaica, I.S.E.R., 1971.

History of the C.P.S.U., Toronto, Progress Books, 1952.

Krupskaya, N.K., *Reminiscences of Lenin*, New York, International, 1970.

Lenin, V.I., *Against Revisionism*, Moscow, F.L.P.H., 1959; *Collected Works*, Moscow, F.L.P.H., 1951; *The Right of Nations to Self-Determination*, Moscow,Progress Publishers, 1968; *Selected Works*, New York, International, 1967, vols.1-3.

Mandel, Ernest, *An Introduction to Marxist Economic Theory*, New York, Merit, 1968; *Revolutionary Strategy in the Imperialist Countries*,New York, Pathfinder,1970.

Morris,George, *The CIA and American Labor,* New York, International, 1967.

Mao Tse-tung, *Selected Works,* London, Lawrence & Wishart, 1954, vols. 1-3.

Robinson, Joan, *The Cultural Revolution in China,* London, Penguin, 1969.

Seale, P. and McConville, Maureen, *French Revolution,1968,* London,Heinemann, 1968.

Schuman, F.L.,*Russia Since 1917,* New York, A.A. Knopf, 1957.

Stalin, J.V.,*Works,* Moscow, F.L.P.H.,1952.

Trotsky, L.D.,*The Death Agony of Capital - ism and the Tasks of the Fourth International,* New York, Pathfinder, 1970; *My Life,* New York, Pathfinder, 1970; *The Permanent Revolution,* New York, Pioneer, 1931; *The Russian Revolution,* New York, Doubleday, 1959; *Stalin,* New York, Harper, 1941.

Wheelwright, E.L. and McFarlane,Bruce, *The Chinese Road to Socialism,* New York,Monthly Review Press, 1970.

Wolfe, B.D., *Three Who Made a Revolution,* New York, Dial Press, 1948.

ARTICLES AND PAMPHLETS, See Notes, especially Chapters, 1, 6, 7.

Index